EDITORS

Vicky Ireland MBE, FRSA was Artistic Director of Polka Theatre, London (1989–2002) and is a Children's Theatre writer and director. She is Co-Artistic Director of A Thousand Cranes Theatre Company. She was awarded an MBE for services to children's drama in 2002, the first of its kind. She has also written for radio and television and has plays published by Nick Hern Books, Dramatic Lines Publishers and Anchorage Press. She instigated children's productions at Regent's Park Open Air Theatre and has directed international productions in Bermuda, Cyprus, Finland, Singapore, Spain, Switzerland, Russia and the Philippines. Vicky is an Honorary Member of TYA-UK and an Honorary Member of ASSITEJ International.

Paul Harman began working as an actor in 1963, became a director of plays and was Artistic Director of Merseyside Young People's Theatre Company (1978–1989) and of Cleveland Theatre Company (1993–2008). He has worked in TYA since 1966 and has staged plays from Bulgaria, Greece, Russia, Quebec, Netherlands, Sweden and Germany, some in his own translations. Paul is Honorary President of TYA-UK and an Honorary Member of ASSITEJ International.

First published in the UK in 2016 by Aurora Metro Publications Ltd.
67 Grove Avenue, Twickenham, TW1 4HX.

info@aurorametro.com   www.aurorametro.com

+44 020 3261 0000

With thanks to: David Broster for initial ideas and Cheryl Robson for her support, encouragement, invaluable editorial comments, and passion for our work.

Thanks also to: Neil Gregory, Ivette Saliba, John McGuire and Sumedha Mane.

Printed by Imprint Digital, UK.
ISBN: 978-1-910798-99-7

50 BEST PLAYS
FOR YOUNG AUDIENCES

**A celebration of 50 years of theatre-making in
England for children and young people**

written and edited by
PAUL HARMAN
AND VICKY IRELAND

AURORA METRO BOOKS

Other books from Aurora Metro
by Paul Harman

A Guide To UK Theatre
For Children and Young Audiences

for our list of plays for young audiences
www.aurorametro.com

We would like to dedicate this book to Stuart Bennett (1937–2015), friend and colleague since our days together at Belgrade TIE. A wonderful mentor, supporter, challenger, inspirer, toiler, leader, bringer-down-to-earth. He led Belgrade TIE and Cockpit TIE, taught Community Theatre at Rose Bruford College, chaired ASSITEJ UK, was Head of Education at V&A's Theatre Museum, archivist for London Drama, organiser of refugee theatre at Hackney Empire, and much more…

CONTENTS

PREFACE

VICKY IRELAND

This book is for students and lovers of theatre, parents and politicians, teachers and actors, a guide to progress over fifty years in a field of theatre dedicated to children and young people. There has been wonderful work created all over the UK but this is very much a personal reflection, based on our careers and our working knowledge of playwriting and production in England.

This book has at its heart a detailed listing of fifty plays by English playwrights chosen by their contemporaries which have most influenced those working professionally to make theatre for young audiences in England today. It describes a journey during which many attitudes towards education and the arts have changed, much has been learned and maybe too much forgotten.

In 2015 we celebrated fifty years of the International Association of Theatre for Children and Young People (known by its French acronym, ASSITEJ). From a handful of European countries ASSITEJ has grown to be a presence in over 80 countries in every continent, promoting the right of every child to experience theatre.

1965 was also the year in which a remarkable and unique experiment combining drama, theatre and education, known as Theatre in Education (TIE), began in the UK, in Coventry. Today, worldwide, practitioners in participatory or immersive theatre are working with children and young people, exploring their real world with them and helping them to express that experience through theatre.

We hope new generations of theatre-makers find this book a useful signpost to sources of inspiration in their future work for young audiences.

July 2016

FOREWORD

SIR KEN ROBINSON

In late July 1984, I was one of several hundred people in an auditorium at Warwick University in the UK, taking part in a unique conference. It was convened by the Arts Council of Great Britain and included members of the country's leading TIE and YPT companies, educators and arts administrators. It was a tense, at times rowdy, affair. In the previous twenty years, TIE had grown from an experimental programme at the Belgrade Theatre in Coventry into an array of several dozen companies, most attached to 'parent' theatres, some free standing. The 'movement', as it was often called, had its own professional association, The Standing Conference of Young People's Theatre, its own journal, conferences and controversies. One of them, which became a focus of the Warwick conference, was whose job it was to pay for it all. This debate was precipitated by general changes in the 1980s in public funding for the arts and for education: it was charged by the perceived anti-establishment programmes and politics of some of SCYPT's members and companies.

As the 80s progressed into the 90s, the funding changes forced the closure of many of these early companies in the UK and new directions in the work of those that survived or came later. Even so, the power, edge and impact of the early TIE/YPT movement continue to reverberate in education and in theatre around the world.

In my experience, TIE/YPT was a very eclectic movement and included a wide range of practices, politics and purposes. The influences on different companies' work included Augusto Boal, Edward Bond, Bertolt Brecht, Peter Brook, Paulo Friere, Ivan Illich, Maria Montessori, Brian Way, Peter Slade and Dorothy Heathcote; and cultural practices from kabuki to commedia dell'arte. For all its diversity, what unified the movement was a shared belief in the power of theatre to transform young peoples' understanding of themselves and of the world around them: and to act accordingly.

For almost fifty years, Vicky Ireland and Paul Harman have been prominent practitioners of and passionate advocates for theatre for young people. Their careers, which span the whole rise and transformation of TIE/YPT, make them uniquely placed to curate this vivid collection of insights on the personalities that shaped the TIE/YPT movement: and of some of its best creative work.

May 2016, Los Angeles

Sir Ken Robinson, PhD is an internationally recognised leader in the development of creativity, innovation and human resources in education and in business.

WHAT ARE TYA & TIE?

PAUL HARMAN

It is usual to assert when writing in England about Theatre for Young Audiences (TYA) that it all began with *Peter Pan*. There may have been earlier plays written expressly for children or for family audiences – there is a distinction between those two categories which not all critics agree upon – but not much is known about them. Or, rather, the academic community has not been sufficiently interested in the field to spend much time looking. Indeed, there are still many critics and writers on theatre who refuse to accept a category of 'Children's Theatre' or 'Theatre for Young Audiences' at all. This book seeks to show that there is indeed a distinct canon of professional writing for young audiences today, and that it has a history, sources, streams, provenance and standards.

So what terms shall we use? Today, following the USA, many people use Theatre for Young Audiences (TYA) to denote theatre presented by adults to children and young people. Theatre in Education (TIE) is best defined in this phrase by Gordon Vallins; 'transformative experiences through the use of theatre techniques that lead to positive learning outcomes'. Those who worked in TIE in the early days were described as 'actor/teachers' to recognise that while performing in role as characters, and usually with the 'audience' in role as well, their task was to provoke positive and thoughtful contributions from all participants in the event.

Other terms used in the 1960s and 70s were 'Children's Theatre', 'Theatre for Young People' (TYP) and 'Young People's Theatre' (YPT). The term 'Youth Theatre' has come to mean theatre created and performed by young people – usually 14+ (National Association of Youth Theatres: www.nayt.org.uk).

However, one of the leading commercial touring companies of the 1950s, founded by the owners of a bombed-out music hall in Birkenhead, was called 'Argyle Theatre for Youth'.

Sadly, 'Children's Theatre' was for a time considered a derogatory term with negative connotations, perhaps linked to snobbish attitudes to 'children's entertainment'. Today the term 'Children's Theatre' can also mean theatre performed *by* children under 12.

Because the first TIE teams were publicly funded by Arts Councils or Education Authorities, the term 'Theatre in Education' gained some extra status. Many small, private companies soon adopted 'Theatre in Education' to mean any kind of performance or drama workshop offered to schools.

An Arts Council policy document of 1986 listed a number of these terms with interpretations which angered some practitioners at the time. But the TIE movement was developing fast and reflecting great upheavals in social attitudes towards sexual orientation and gender identity, disability and inclusion, race and multiculturalism. For example, race- and gender-blind or integrated casting was practised and explored way ahead of the adult theatre of the time. Perhaps the authorities were just unable to keep up.

1965 to 2015

We have been spurred to mark two particular anniversaries with this book. The first celebrates the inauguration of the Belgrade Theatre in Education (TIE) Company at Coventry in 1965. A generation of young educationalists and theatre-makers passed through that new institution, a remarkable innovation, and went on to create and strongly influence many of the key professional theatre companies dedicated to theatre for young audiences today. (See article by Gordon Vallins on Belgrade Theatre in Education.)

Also in 1965 the International Association of Theatre for Children and Young People (ASSITEJ) was founded. Today ASSITEJ links professional colleagues in over 80 countries in all continents. Its work ensures that plays and productions flow with increasing freedom across the world, especially at the growing number of well-resourced international festivals.

At these international events, UK artists and their work can be promoted and also challenged by their peers. The question of whether theatre is a universal or culturally determined art form is naturally raised in such encounters. As is discussed in a later article, different conditions can lead to very different approaches. But we must also make the reader aware that the plays selected for this book mainly represent what has developed in England over the last fifty years.

Governments in Scotland, Wales and Northern Ireland are increasingly autonomous and have long had their own approaches to funding and managing the arts and education. They have their own traditions of playwriting and specific cultural contexts which inform the plays they make for children and young people. In Wales, for example, a determined effort was made over decades to ensure that every child received regular experiences of theatre delivered by a locally based TIE company, free of charge. Indeed, many of us struggling in England were very jealous of the security enjoyed by our colleagues in Wales – until another change in UK national policy, sad to say, evened up the misery! Cwmni Theatr Arad Goch celebrates both national and international work in its festival Agor Drysau – Opening Doors (www.aradgoch.cymru).

In Scotland, Imaginate built on the foundation of an annual international festival of TYA and is now a development agency known and respected around the world (www.imaginate.org.uk).

No part of the UK has seen greater change in the last fifty years than Northern Ireland where peace has come after a long period of division. TYA companies and artists throughout the island of Ireland now find it natural to work together. Young at Art and Belfast Children's Festival led the way (www.youngatart.co.uk) alongside the Baboro Arts Festival for Children in Galway (www.baboro.ie) and the Sticky Fingers Early Years Arts Festival in Newry (www.stickyfingersarts.co.uk).

Democracy in Culture

We have tried in our selection of texts to choose plays which exemplify key trends, turning points, contexts and influences and the changes in themes and topics as the years passed. In particular, many of the earlier plays were written for and performed by companies of professional actors in schools, rather than in theatres.

In 1960s England, the openness of schools to the arts was the remarkable achievement of a generation of artists and politicians keen to democratise Culture. This was embodied in the 1944 Education Act, which sought to make a genuinely liberal education available to all and in the creation in 1946 of the Arts Council of Great Britain to provide government funding for the arts for the first time.

Bertha Waddell's Children's Theatre was founded in 1927 in Scotland by sisters Bertha and Jenny Waddell. It was the first UK professional theatre company that was solely for children and in the mid-1930s a Glasgow Director of Education allowed her company to perform in junior schools within school time. The Scottish Theatre Archive notes material recording events in 1929; 'Friday and Saturday matinees featuring a programme of folk-songs, nursery rhymes, plays, dance and mime. The principal item on the programme was a playlet entitled *The Poor Princess*.'

From the 1940s, Esme Church's work at the Young Vic in London and in Bradford in the north of England attracted attention and touring companies were becoming regular features of school life.

In the 1940s and 50s, Caryl Jenner at Unicorn, Brian Way at Theatre Centre and a tiny handful of other pioneers in the emerging movement of educators, such as Peter Slade, committed to the introduction to schools of Drama in Education, were laying the foundations for new kinds of theatre for children and young people.

The explosion of TIE and TYA in the 1960s was possible only because of a further change in the political climate – in 1964 for the first time the UK Government appointed a Minister for the Arts. The 1965 White Paper introduced by Jennie Lee MP secured a significant change in emphasis.

Where before the national Arts Council had spent the largest part of its modest government funding to support the elite Royal Opera House in London, now local authorities, like the City of Coventry, were supported to build new theatres and take the arts to the people. TIE was made possible in provincial towns and cities like Wigan, Rochdale, Hull, Norwich, Leeds, Watford and Newcastle by new money and new politics.

And there were actors, teachers, writers and designers, willing to explore these new opportunities with enthusiasm.

Participation

Audience participation has long been a feature of popular theatre. Catcalls and comments from the audience may be discouraged among serious middle-class theatre-goers, respectful of the artist's work. The hush expected in an art gallery or concert hall and outrage over the use of mobile phones during performances come naturally to those 'educated' in the protocol associated with certain kinds of arts experiences. But for many people, performers are there to spark a response from those who have paid for the experience.

We must suppose that the atmosphere at the Globe in Shakespeare's time was not always reverent. Down the years since then, theatres have been places where all kinds of behaviour may have been tolerated and even expected.

In keeping with the desire to reach a wider public than those 'educated' to behave respectfully in the presence of art, the pioneers of the new kind of theatre celebrated in this book embraced audience participation in all its forms.

In the British pantomime tradition, based on the nineteenth-century music hall and variety shows, audiences are expected to hiss and boo at the villain and cheer the hero. The cross-dressing in panto is of course another tradition with much earlier roots in folk ceremonies and entertainments.

The new generation of theatre-makers therefore explored every kind of audience participation, from popular theatre traditions of shouting out warnings to the characters on stage like; 'He's behind you!' to intensive immersion, site-specific events and shows influenced by performance art.

Those who were strongly influenced by educational theory believed in the maxim attributed to Confucius; 'I hear and I forget. I see and I remember. **I do and I understand.**' For them, any deeper understanding of what is happening in the theatre event demands that the spectator also takes on a role in the proceedings and has an attitude which is both validated and challenged.

It may be argued that in any good play, well-performed, we laugh and cry when directed. In a TIE event, the actor/teachers may deliberately seek to draw young people into an emotional engagement with a character or an argument, only to challenge it later. This is to show the complexity of an issue or to underline how hard it may be to sustain a position. But the physical embodiment of an argument, in which two or more sides are emotionally engaged, is more memorable than a purely intellectual presentation.

It must also be remembered that during the period when the most radical TIE teams were active, serious public issues affecting in particular the 'working classes' – the majority of the people – were at stake.

TIE companies sought both to recover the history of working people, as opposed to the history of elites, and also to make young people aware of their right and duty to engage in struggles for greater liberty and equality in society.

These are not neutral but highly contentious issues. It may be taken as natural that children are encouraged to cheer on a hero or even make the physical motions of rowing him to safety, or blow to fill his sails when that hero is the mythical Odysseus. When that hero is a mutineer, a miner or the victim of pollution by an industry, the boundary between exploration and advocacy of a political position becomes harder to determine.

In the 1980s and 1990s, UK politicians became aware that contentious issues were being treated not only in theatre programmes but also in other parts of the school's activity. They intervened both to require that a more formal, regulated approach to education take precedence over the informal or experiential approaches to learning favoured from the 1960s, but also, at the extreme, to enact prescriptive legislation.

Most notably, Section 28 of the Local Government Act 1988 prohibited local authorities from 'promoting' homosexuality or gay 'pretended family relationships', and prevented Councils spending money on educational materials and projects perceived to promote a gay lifestyle.

Several TIE teams were challenged for the content of their work. David Johnston writes in a 1983 edition of NADECT's magazine, *Outlook*, that Norman Tebbit, a prominent Conservative MP, had sought to have Theatre Centre banned from schools in Waltham Forest, because they dealt with a 'peace' theme.

TIE and the Left

This is not the place to discuss in detail the differences of approach in relation to politics and social issues between practitioners of theatre for young audiences over the last fifty years. But some remarks are essential to indicate the strength of commitment shown by many on the Left to the empowerment of young people through theatre.

From the 1970s, a strong UK movement of community and political theatre emerged, similarly motivated to movements elsewhere in Europe after 1968. This is recorded in the work of *Unfinished Histories* (www.unfinishedhistories.com). The Independent Theatre Council (ITC) was formed to provide a vehicle for learning and mutual support, representation and solidarity among the many new companies, including TYA companies.

The TIE movement came together within the Standing Conference of Young People's Theatres (SCYPT). This writer's own pound note, slapped on a table to signal a commitment to common action in favour of high-quality theatre for young people, may have been one step on the journey. Later, a group of practitioners closely associated with the Workers Revolutionary Party, which was active in theatre circles then, and most notably supported by Vanessa and Corin Redgrave, sought to mandate a single line of approach to the work. Clashes were inevitable.

The annual SCYPT conference week was an invaluable chance to share ideas, see each other's work and develop a sense of community and common purpose. SCYPT journals were a platform for debate and information. Today, annual events like the Takeoff Festival, founded by David Johnston in 1988, play a similar but less coherent role in the continuing development of the work.

Over the last seventeen years, Edward Bond, a great writer whose work is strongly infused with Left politics, has written many plays for Big Brum Theatre. Its website states: 'The company uses theatre and drama alongside young people to make meaning of their lives and the world around them. The work has a strong theoretical basis: focusing artistically on the power of theatre images and dramatic action to create resonances and challenge us to new ways of thinking, whilst being educationally grounded in active learning and problem-solving.'

Bond was sufficiently respected by Arts Council England that he was invited to give the keynote speech at a major conference, "What is good children's theatre?" But his plays for young people have not been widely presented in the UK.

An objective history of SCYPT, Left politics and their influence on TYA remains to be written.

By the 2000s, with the demise of the core TIE companies in England, thanks to the gradual withdrawal of public funding, the UK Centre of ASSITEJ became the only body to represent the field now known as TYA.

Social Changes

With the rise in general prosperity over fifty years a theatre ticket has become more affordable for many, although many companies report falling attendances and fewer bookings by schools in recent years. There is a growing inequality in theatre as elsewhere in Britain and many other changes to our culture which affect the role theatre plays in our lives.

There have been big physical changes to that first wave of new theatres built in the 1960s. In Coventry, the Belgrade Theatre has doubled in size with the addition of a studio theatre and many more offices for new departments of public engagement, marketing and management. Theatres in other cities, like Leeds, Birmingham and Leicester are on their second or third refurbishment or rebuild.

But they are usually producing fewer new shows than they did fifty years ago. There may be more money for buildings but not for actors!

Few of the specialist TYA or TIE companies have survived from the 1960s while the names of others have changed as companies took a new direction.

For example, in North East England, Cleveland Theatre Company built on Billingham Forum's 1960s work in schools and is now Theatre Hullabaloo, which today does much more work in theatres.

Playwright David Wood's Whirligig touring company completed twenty-five years success in negotiating space for children within the national network of commercial theatres but finally withdrew. (See the article by David Wood in *Theatre for Children and Young People*, ed. Stuart Bennett. Aurora Metro)

Changes in the way schools are run and funded killed off a number of the strongest Theatre in Education (TIE) companies in the 1990s, including Belgrade TIE itself which closed in 1996. By contrast, Leeds TIE, one of the earliest and most radical of companies, is still led by two of its original members, Annalyn Bhanji and Paul Swift.

In the early days, Local Authorities could use education funds to pay for a free service of theatre in schools. Later, Central Government reduced the power of Local Authorities and devolved funding to schools. That meant theatre companies had to sell their productions to each school individually. The concept of a free service run as a partnership between theatre people and teachers was hard to sustain.

While Theatre in Education teams used theatre and participatory drama methods as tools to deliver wider educational aims, today's TYA companies, if they receive public funding at all, are either funded by Arts Councils to deliver artistic aims or by agencies, such as the NHS, to promote specific campaigns or messages.

Naturally there have been other developments in response to a changing society. Theatre Mobile left Burnley to become M6 Theatre in Rochdale after a particularly challenging production ruffled local feathers.

Touring or Building-Based?

While most UK TYA companies still tour to venues or schools, in recent years a number of companies have settled in dedicated theatre spaces, aiming to create optimum conditions for showing their work.

In the early 1960s John English had imaginative plans to establish a permanent theatre for children in a Birmingham park – now known as MAC, the Midlands Arts Centre. Richard Gill was next in 1979 with the child-centred conversion of a former church hall in Wimbledon as a home for his Polka Theatre. Unicorn Theatre began as a touring company, settled in London in 1961 at the Arts Theatre in Newport Street, Covent Garden, and now has a magnificent, purpose-built theatre near Tower Bridge.

Half Moon Young People's Theatre was established by the Inner London Education Authority during the mid-1970s as the specialist youth and schools' arm of the Half Moon Repertory Theatre, producing youth theatre productions, specialist training programmes and participatory Theatre in Education for schools. With the appointment of the present Director Chris Elwell in 1997, the company underwent a radical re-focusing of operations. Half Moon is now a fully accessible, purpose-converted theatre building.

In 2005, Kate Cross, Head of Education at Theatre Royal Bath, persuaded her Board to buy an adjacent building and create a dedicated space for young people, now known as 'the egg'. In 2015, Plymouth City Council approved Stiltskin Theatre's plan to transform a building in Devonport Park into an 80-seat children's theatre with an outdoor amphitheatre seating up to 500 people.

The latest dedicated TYA venue is in Darlington for Theatre Hullabaloo, which stages the annual TakeOff Festival (www. takeofffestival.org.uk). The Hullaballoon, a flagship venue for young audiences in Darlington, will open in 2017.

However, Liverpool's Everyman Theatre, which first received public funding as a 'young people's theatre' has long since become a venue with an adult programme. Contact Theatre in Manchester has changed its clientele over the years and is now serving a wide range of demographics and communities. John English's Midland Arts Centre for Young People, which inspired me so strongly in 1962, is now a rather more grown-up, even chic, MAC.

Touring companies still predominate. Natalie Wilson at Theatre Centre, London, Jude Merrill at Travelling Light in Bristol, Wendy Harris, at Tutti-Frutti in Leeds and Nicki Sved at Theatre Alibi in Exeter are leading commissioners and producers of new writing and excellent plays, designed in all respects for mobility, intimacy of scale and sensitivity to the needs of young audiences.

With Adel Al-Salloum, Director of The Spark Festival in Leicester, Dot Wood at M6, Nina Hajiyianni at Action Transport, Miranda Thain at Hullabaloo, Deborah Pakkar-Hull at Theatre Company Blah Blah Blah, Sarah Brigham at Derby Theatre, Daphna Attias at Peut-Être, Tina Williams at Pied Piper, Teresa Aristio at Company of Angels, and Purni Morell at Unicorn, many of the key companies are today led by women. (By contrast, few women playwrights feature in our selection of plays.)

The companies mentioned above are currently among the fortunate ones, with regular public funding to enable them to experiment and commission new writing.

Most of the more than 100 independent companies travelling the roads of Britain, from hall to hall and from school to school, are tiny ensembles of dedicated people, bringing well-known stories or explorations of science and history to audiences of children who would otherwise never have an experience of live theatre.

The Bottom Line

Despite the success of so many professional companies reaching so many children and young people, the underlying financial facts have stayed the same over fifty years.

We may desire to create and deliver a theatre experience of the same quality as that expected by adults and take it to every child, but the reality is that the cash available is much less, in the amount which parents and schools will pay for a child's ticket or which the public purse will supply.

One key decision of principle to make is the size of audience you believe most appropriate for a given show or age range. The smaller the audience, the closer they can all be to the action. That makes for a more intense experience but limits the amount you can earn from selling tickets.

For the artists making theatre there are always frustrations: you simply cannot deliver a theme or idea which demands more resources than you can afford. With less money to spend than in the adult theatre, casts are usually smaller and the amount a writer can earn from his or her work is much smaller too – unless you are very prolific or very lucky. Most plays in our selection are for small numbers of actors.

In short, professional artists cannot offer a quality experience to every child if government, parents or schools won't pay their wages.

TIE and TYA have changed over the years as fashions in theatre have changed – and so have schools. But certain principles have stuck. Most theatre made for young audiences in the UK still seeks to address the needs of the individual child, taking account of the stage of social, emotional, intellectual and physical development it has attained.

We hope this selection of texts and related articles succeeds in persuading the reader that TIE and TYA in England have a history to be proud of – and a future.

THE PIONEERS

PAUL HARMAN

Certain names stand out in the list of those most important to the early development of TIE and TYA in the UK. Three of them created their own theatre companies and unique styles of theatre production based on a firmly held conception of what children deserved to see as their first experience of professional performing arts.

Caryl Jenner (1928–1973)

Caryl Jenner was influenced by a principle upheld in many European countries, such as France, Germany or the former USSR: that all children should be introduced to the arts as part of their cultural heritage. Essentially, Jenner aspired to offer the same standards and production values as adults would expect. While the content of the plays she commissioned were tailored to the age and experience of children in the audience, perhaps the expectations of their theatre-going parents determined the style of theatre she espoused. After years of touring she fought for a theatre space of her own, among the West End theatres which set our standards in the 1950s.

From 1944 Caryl Jenner wrote Christmas Pantomimes for small playhouses. During performances she would make note of the behaviour of the children, recording what scenes and sequences held their attention, and which did not. She began to formulate the principles that would guide her theatre and writing.

In 1947 the 'Mobile Theatre' was born. Caryl's mission was to drive around the austere post-war towns of Britain, as well as isolated villages, to bring theatre to new audiences. They supplemented their income by performing to adults in the evenings but their goal was always to captivate the minds and imagination of children.

The 'Mobile Theatre' continued to grow in reputation, gaining success and acclaim. In 1950 it changed its name to 'The Caryl Jenner Mobile Theatre', to signify Caryl's influence. In 1962, the name changed again, to the 'Unicorn Theatre Club'.

In 1967, the company gave up touring and, on receiving a £10,000 annual grant from the Arts Council, took up a lease at the Arts Theatre in London, which remained its home until the present Unicorn Theatre was built in 2005.

Caryl Jenner died in January 1973 at the age of 55. She left behind a theatre with national acclaim and a clear set of artistic principles.

Richard Gill

Richard Gill founded Polka Theatre – and created a delightful, child-centred building as its home – to feature puppetry in full-scale, drama productions, mainly adaptations of traditional stories. In choosing the suburb of Wimbledon rather than Central London for his permanent theatre, he showed a commitment to the idea that each theatre, wherever it is based, should develop its own audience, ethos and style. He was influenced by the best models of state-funded puppet companies in Eastern Europe.

Polka Theatre started life as a touring company in 1967 under Richard's Artistic Directorship. Gill was spurred on by a commitment to fine design and craftsmanship and a passion for puppetry, taking the company's work to many of Britain's major theatres. By 1971, following a successful Arts Council application (the first annual grant to any company working in the field of puppetry), Polka was attracting staggering audiences of 250,000 each year.

But touring to other people's theatres imposed restrictions: small casts, shows that will fit every stage. Gill had a policy of bringing skill, craft and colour to Polka's productions, and now he wanted to do the same to a building which could be a home for Polka's work. In 1976, Polka found the Holy Trinity Halls in Wimbledon and in 1979, following a lengthy fundraising campaign, Polka's dream of a permanent home for children's theatre became a reality.

When Polka – The Children's Theatre opened its doors on 20th November 1979, it became the UK's first theatre venue dedicated exclusively to children. This momentous event was marked by a Gala Performance attended by Her Majesty Queen Elizabeth the Queen Mother.

With two performance spaces, a 300-seat main auditorium and a 90-seat studio), a café, a playground, a toy shop and exhibition and gallery spaces, Polka Theatre was unique in its totally child-centred design. It quickly became a popular attraction both locally and London-wide, for the high production values of its ongoing programme of puppetry performances, and for the exceptional environment in which they were staged.

By 1983 Polka was regularly programming and producing productions aimed specifically at the under-5s alongside its productions for ages 6–12. The studio, known as the Adventure Theatre, became the designated performance space, and even today it remains the only space in the UK dedicated exclusively to work for Early Years audiences.

Brian Way (1923–2006)

Brian Way created Theatre Centre as a national touring vehicle for a style of arena theatre based on his understanding of child development. His book Development through Drama was a key influence on a generation of TIE pioneers. Theatre Centre has never had a permanent theatre house as its base.

THE PIONEERS

Brian Way established Theatre Centre in London in 1953. The company originated the modern concept of theatre for children in an educational context.

He was the prime mover in a group of lecturers and teachers who were in 1946 considering the relationship between theatre and teaching. People such as Peter Slade, Warren Jenkins and John English had a considerable influence on his thinking and he edited Slade's book *Child Drama*. They worked together at Bristol Old Vic, where he met his first wife, Kathleen. After his marriage to her in 1946, they came to London and he continued to make a rather tenuous living from lecturing and teaching until the beginning of the 1950s, when he provided a centre for unemployed actors, on occasional days, at a hall in Loudoun Road, St John's Wood.

There he produced plays in the round including *Philoctetes*, *Pinocchio*, which he wrote with Warren Jenkins in 1951, and an abbreviated version of *The Man Born to be King* by Dorothy L. Sayers. Sayers herself saw this production and was so impressed she donated £200 so that he could establish Theatre Centre as a company, whose board of management she joined. Brian, who had co-founded the West Country Children's Theatre Company after the war, again turned his attention to educational children's theatre.

He and Margaret Faulkes, in founding Theatre Centre in London, introduced the concept of informal theatrical performances in school, and the expansion of arts education. He believed that plays in this context ought to be performed in the round, for specific age groups limited in number, with professional actors capable of interacting with the children.

He engaged professional actors who understood children and education, who interacted with them and worked in small, well-rehearsed companies that travelled nationally from school to school.

Nationwide, this heresy became increasingly successful with enlightened Directors of Education – despite opposition from traditionalists, who were then probably in a majority.

Brian believed that plays should be entertaining, as well as informative. In 1966 Theatre Centre began to receive Arts Council support and on one occasion Brian had to be restrained from encouraging the then chairman of the Arts Council, Lord Goodman, to participate on all fours in a play for eight-year-olds. But then he considered it patronising to refer to children as kids, and cared more for the dignity of the child than the dignity of the adult.

His work ranged far beyond direction and his seminal textbooks, Development through Drama (1967) and Audience Participation (1981), have been translated into many languages.

He retired from Theatre Centre in 1977 and became a visiting professor in a number of distinguished universities, moving permanently to Canada in 1983.

The Arts Council of Great Britain established The Children's Award to celebrate the accomplishments and raise the profile of theatre for young people and most especially playwrights who work in this field. Since 2008 Theatre Centre has administrated this Award, which has been renamed 'The Brian Way Award' in honour and recognition of this pioneering man of extraordinary vision.

Cecil Philip Taylor (1929–1981)

C.P. Taylor was born in Glasgow, but his playwriting career began after a move to Newcastle upon Tyne in 1955. He wrote more than 70 plays and screenplays, including *And A Nightingale Sang...* (1978) and *Good* (1981). His work has played on Broadway, in the West End and in a major retrospective at the Edinburgh International Festival.

Like his other plays for young audiences, *Operation Elvis* emerged from a lengthy project focusing on children with the Tyneside Theatre Company, and later, Northumberland Experimental Youth Theatre. Taylor described his technique as "tuning into an audience ... to give me an understanding of the children, their culture and subculture all basically leading to a good two-way, mutually respectful relationship."

This tuning-in moved beyond traditional Theatre in Education practices to encompass gathering young people's written reflections on their daily lives, interviewing them one-on-one and in small groups, embarking on ethnographic 'walkabouts' with children in their local areas, including home visits, and arranging workshops with professional actors and directors.

Taylor's son Avram, in a fascinating article about his father's career, states that his innovatory methods "successfully manage to deal with some of the children's own prejudices: racism, preconceptions about those with learning disabilities, and attitudes to poverty in the Third World, while not preaching or shrinking from the harsh realities of those issues."

As Susan Friesner has noted, Taylor's plays were "remarkable for their time in that they deal with serious social issues and are written from the unsentimental standpoint that children's relationships are as complicated as those of adults."

Taylor himself liked to reverse this statement, declaring that; "I try to make my plays for children as rewarding for adults so that they can be the shared experience all good theatre is."

Despite the move away from the traditional TIE model, productions such as Operation Elvis nonetheless toured to schools rather than theatres. The original Malcolm, Tim Healy, recalls: "We did 90 performances in eight weeks. We'd go to a school, unload the van, put the set up, do the play, knock it down and onto the next school … and they were the happiest days of my life."

From an article by Ben Fletcher-Watson (Royal Conservatoire of Scotland)

John Allen (1923–2002)

John Allen played a prominent role in the development of drama and dance education, after an early career in avant garde theatre. In the 1940s he led Glyndebourne Children's Theatre. He was appointed HM Inspector of Schools with national responsibility for drama and dance in 1961, at a time when those activities were very much poor relations in school curricula. He had a passionate belief in the value of performance in personal development, and in the importance of teaching standards.

John English (1911–1998)

After a career as an industrial chemist, John English retired aged 40 and devoted himself to theatre.

In 1948, he founded the Arena Theatre Company, a small, professional touring company which aimed to explore and develop how to introduce theatre to young people. They also provided theatre to areas in both the city and across the country where theatre was less prominent, thus bringing it to the masses. As well as experimenting with new, different forms of theatre and presentation, they would perform 'under canvas' (a circus tent) in the summer and with the help of the Arts Council they were able to take performing arts to places that were without a theatre. English's wife, Mollie Randle later mentioned in an interview that the Arena Theatre's main practice was 'of touring Birmingham parks in the summer and halls around the country in the winter, the theatre performed a range of popular plays and classics for adults and children's plays'.

One of those plays was Brian Way's *Pinocchio*.

In 1960, English with his wife Mollie Randle and Councillor Sir Frank Price proposed the creation of an arts centre to the members of Birmingham City Council. In 1962, the council donated a site in Cannon Hill Park for the sole use of the Midlands Arts Centre for Young People, now known as MAC.

It would be a place to allow younger people to experience a wider range of art forms as well as their practises and traditions.

Building work was completed in the mid-1960s and with two small theatres and studios it was the first centre of its kind in Britain. It also housed the Cannon Hill Puppet Theatre under John M. Blundall. MAC was given a £15m renovation and re-opened in 2010.

Fellow Travellers

We should also record some pioneers whose names are less frequently found in on-line searches today.

Gerald Tyler was a Drama Adviser in the educationally progressive West Riding of Yorkshire who inspired the young Patrick Stewart to become an actor. While serving as UK representative at an ITI (International Theatre Institute) gathering, his conversations with eminent specialists in TYA from Russia and France led to the setting up of ASSITEJ after an inaugural session in London.

Noël Greig (1944–2009) and **Geoff Gillham** (1946–2001) made contributions to the development of TYA and TIE which are highly valued today by those who worked with them.

Many early TIE practitioners and companies were indebted to the inspiration of drama pioneers like **Gavin Bolton** or **Dorothy Heathcote**.

In the early days, the craft was mostly learned by doing, from observing fellow actor/teachers or from taking advantage of opportunities to see companies from abroad on rare visits to festivals.

Some members of the early companies became today's successful writers of plays for young audiences.

But first a movement had to be launched…

THEATRE IN EDUCATION IS BORN

GORDON VALLINS

Gordon Vallins joined the Belgrade in 1964. A year later he ushered in a completely new approach to engaging young people in theatre.

TIE was born in Coventry in 1965 on Wednesday 15th September at the John Gulson Primary School, George Street with Junior Programme One, a devised programme called *The Secret of the Stone.* There was no thought at that moment of a future beyond making sure the enterprise worked well. Little did we four – Ann Lister, Jessica Hill, Dickon Reed (the first to be called actor/teachers), and myself as producer/teacher, together with Janet Mattock, our part-time secretary and Jonathan Ellis our young driver/technician – have any idea we were sparking off an international movement. A movement that now is the subject of academic study, related publications, and GCSE and BTEC examinations. Practising companies in 2015 may now be found on the world-wide web.

One: A little background

Fifty years ago it was a different world: TV was black and white, no DVDs, music was played on vinyl and tapes. There were no mobile phones, no lap tops, no readily available photo copiers. The 'white heat of the technological revolution' as announced by Prime Minister Harold Wilson in 1963 was in its infancy.

THEATRE IN EDUCATION IS BORN

For us the time was optimistic. The Beatles and the Stones vied for *Top of the Pops*. Sean Connery as James Bond became an iconic heart-throb. The BBC aired the first episode of *Doctor Who*. In fashion there was Mary Quant and the miniskirt. The contraceptive pill became universally available. And in 1964 Labour appointed the first minister for the Arts. Radical changes were taking place politically, culturally and socially.

In 1965 the Belgrade was seven years old. It was the first professional and civic theatre to be built after World War II. The centre of Coventry had been devastated by Nazi bombing and the City was determined to rebuild. A new cathedral grew beside the bombed shell of the old one, a traffic-free shopping centre emerged, together with new comprehensive schools and a theatre named after its twinned Yugoslavian city in the spirit of European reconstruction.

As one of its two annual twelve-week repertoire seasons, The Belgrade Theatre Company, for its seventh birthday celebrations, mounted Anouilh's historical drama *Beckett*; Shakespeare's *Taming of the Shrew*; a new play by David Turner – *Bottomley*,[1] T.S. Eliot's *The Cocktail Party*; *Oh! What a Lovely War* and a specially devised piece: *Out of the Ashes*, about wartime Coventry and Coventry's survival.

Published in the programme accompanying the celebratory season, is stated the Belgrade "will provide a scheme of theatre education for Coventry schools". There was also an announcement of building a theatre annexe for rehearsals and work with young people. Sir Laurence Olivier laid the foundation stone. (He was appearing in the National Theatre's production of Ibsen's *The Master Builder* at the nearby (now defunct) Coventry Theatre).

At that time I was Assistant to the Director. The hook had been the opportunity to direct plays.[2] In effect the actual job comprised of press and public relations, (writing press releases, hosting first nights), reading new play scripts, conducting coach parties on tours round the theatre, giving talks to clubs and societies, standing in for the manager on his nights off, auditioning actors, helping to plan programmes and liaising with schools and the city's education department. And it was the latter area of responsibility that proved the most interesting and challenging.[3]

When I arrived at the Belgrade the prime aim was to get young people into the auditorium. Here lie the roots of TIE. There had been previous attempts to find ways of encouraging the young – Theatre Holiday sessions at Easter and Christmas, also a young supporters club, who could claim reduced admission, and a schools' touring programme called *Theatre as Entertainment*.

Time had elapsed and activity had been suspended; the only remaining theatre opportunity for young people were two annual matinee performances of suitable plays funded by the Local Education Authority. On the afternoons of a Shakespeare play, the auditorium packed with unprepared talkative teenagers who, to announce their appreciation, spun polo mints onto the stage. Actors loathed it and presented some of the quickest Shakespeare ever.

After an evaluation of the situation the young supporters club was revived with holiday workshops and the inauguration of a youth theatre; the talks to schools became drama lessons, also the establishment of weekly evening drama classes in a nearby school's dining room and, for the youth theatre, a rehearsal space was made available at a local college of further education. At this time too, contact was made with Coventry College of Education where the drama department was led by Walter Ellis. He became a very welcome, on-going mentor to the theatre's educational work and his observations and perceptive comments were thoughtful and encouraging; he also encouraged his students (teachers in training) to share the organisation and leadership roles of workshops and holiday activities.

Two: Preparation for TIE

TIE's major stimulus and inspiration was the Belgrade's Artistic Director, Anthony Richardson, a true theatre visionary, and were it not for his perseverance and political manoeuvring, belligerent enthusiasm, charming insistence and ability to persuade the Belgrade Theatre Trust, City Councillors, the City Treasurer and the Education Officers, the original scheme would never have come into being.

Richardson embraced ideas. He saw the theatre making a direct contribution to the life of the city. He described theatre as a social necessity and himself as a community servant. He was not just interested in schools – he also wanted theatre to embrace working men's clubs and factories, the law, social services, art galleries, Rotary clubs and business. He wished to see every aspect of city life somehow involved with theatre.

I did take *Maria Marten*, with its music-hall songs to working men's clubs, successful in itself but lacking a real awareness and understanding of the situation and possibilities of future development.

The 1960s was also the period of the struggles of Arnold Wesker to establish his dream of a working class cultural centre at London's Roundhouse, and Joan Littlewood's Fun Palace in London's East End. Both projects remained largely on the drawing board due to lack of funding. The Belgrade's search for embracing the city of Coventry in cultural experiences, while sharing a similar philosophy, eventually made partial successful headway with TIE.

On a train journey with Richardson to a meeting of CORT (Council of Repertory Theatres) in London we discussed ways of setting up theatre for children, recognising that in the ten years of compulsory schooling (then 5–15) theatre should play a fundamental and important part in the school's curriculum. He asked me to get the ideas we discussed down on paper.

The resultant memorandum, *Belgrade Theatre and Education* suggested learning structures for primary and secondary schools, including practical, active drama workshops organised by the theatre in, and out, of school time; we envisaged day schools in radio and TV studios, the Coventry Herbert Art Gallery on theatre design, influential periods of history and costume and social behaviour, residential courses for school leavers, and courses for teachers. Young people would be encouraged to create their own theatre. A Theatre for Children was to be established and, once a year, the Belgrade would mount the most demanding, exciting specially devised and written theatre event imaginable. The courses were to be linked, never isolated. In the course of discussion it was felt Theatre and Education were two separate ideas when in fact the ideas should be indivisible so 'in' replaced the 'and', and thus the scheme became known as *Theatre in Education.*[4]

In the autumn of 1964 David Turner, playwright and theatre adviser, Richardson and myself, the Chairman of the Belgrade Theatre Trust and Chairman of the Education Committee met to discuss the proposal. The outcome was encouraging. At the time it was possible for local authorities to levy up to sixpence on the rates for artistic enterprise. The councillors reckoned a penny on the rate would raise £50,000. We couldn't believe our luck.

Richardson was interviewed by the *Guardian*, and he discussed his hopes of a co-operative complex of Midland theatres sharing resources, productions and audiences; he also mentioned the Belgrade initiative for a theatre education scheme, new to this country, that would cost £50,000 (nearer to £700,000 in 2015) a year. When the article was published I believe it was the first time the City Treasurer's office had heard of it.

Hasty clandestine meetings were called. Further memoranda followed, mostly concerned with finance. The budget of £15,000 (nearer to £200,000 in 2015) was eventually suggested as possible. This meant the working out of a reduced programme. We had yet to get agreement from head teachers and the Chief Education Officer. I was asked to write a further memorandum. It was hoped this second memorandum, *Theatre in Education II*, headed by a quotation from The City of Coventry's Civic Handbook 1964/65 would prick the Council's conscience into supporting The Belgrade's foray into education:

> "The Company shall in the conduct of its affairs to have regard for the desirability of assisting the Council in its capacity as the Local Education Authority in the development of appreciation of drama in the schools of the city."

What now evolved was a tighter structure. TIE was to be:

1) an inspirational teaching service for practising teachers,

2) the establishment of a flexible children's theatre company of nine able to teach and act for young people at each level,

and

3) An advisory service, organising courses, including personal advice and guidance on school productions, loan of equipment not usually found in schools, lamps, sound effects, assorted rostra, possible scenic units etc., also a library of potential dramatic material, plays, stories, tape recordings, etc.

Richardson argued that if £150,000 could be made available for the year commencing April 1965, the Belgrade Theatre could provide a children's theatre company of nine artists plus related teaching materials, with the idea the full scheme would come into operation as monies become available. The Chief Education Officer organised a meeting between The Belgrade Theatre and head-teachers, out of which an advisory panel was formed. What attracted the head-teachers was the funding for the TIE project would *not* come out of their own school budgets but be directly funded by the City Council.

Adverts were placed in the national press for Head of Department and Actor/Teacher assistants. Eventually three actor/teachers were appointed, but no head of department in post, to prepare for, and to work in schools in the Autumn Term when it had been announced the scheme would begin. Sensing an embarrassing hiatus I was asked if I would take temporary responsibility for a pilot programme. I agreed but with little idea of what could possibly be achieved except having a belief in four determined and active minds coming up with answers and collectively structure a workable programme.

Research was essential. A plan of action was drawn up that involved meeting the three appointees, writing to publishers for educational and dramatic material, visiting schools, talking with teachers and meeting head-teachers individually.

And whilst there was an understanding of how secondary schools worked, I had limited knowledge of infant and junior schools and the interests and capabilities of the 5–11 year olds and the possibilities each school might offer in terms of ideas and spaces.

I purposefully set out to discuss plans and ways of working with Brian Way[5] whom I had met when teaching and recognised as possibly the most valuable source of ideas and experience. Through his own work in schools, he had formulated a practical working pattern and, whilst the content and style of TIE work would be different, there would be initially organisational and philosophical similarities. We, and the TIE teams who followed, would be indebted to his interest and input. It was a busy summer.

Three: Establishing TIE

They were raw, proud days, full of argument, invention, decision making and work with a high proportion of in-built job satisfaction. And I was determined that the four of us should work as a team with shared decision making, recognising that each of us had a degree of individual related specialism. Our aims were clear: "to provide an inspirational teaching service and to discover ways of combining theatre techniques with current progressive educational methods". In other words, the pilot scheme set out to transform the learning situation into a three dimensional interactive experience appropriate to the age range and abilities of the young people in the classroom, the school hall, the youth club and the theatre. I was determined from the outset that TIE was not about youngsters acquiring theatre skills or indeed encouraging theatre going. That would perhaps come later. It was about the possibilities of creating transformative experiences through the use of theatre techniques that lead to positive learning outcomes.

Each programme was specially devised for specific age ranges and levels of ability and set out to engage young minds with ideas, issues and concepts and complexities of the living situation.

For the success of the scheme we needed the confidence, co-operation and advice of the teachers whose schools were involved. From the outset teachers were consulted, the work described and, if possible, demonstrated and this process of consultation was recognised as an important aspect of programming.

Generally, with very few exceptions, the teachers, after some initial suspicions, were enthusiastic in their response. The pilot scheme proved successful and formed a practical starting point for all that followed.

At that time, the thought occurred that we were working hopefully towards redundancy; we could, after two or three years, go elsewhere, beyond Coventry. What we thought might happen is that two or more teachers would form their own school's TIE team and set up their own learning programmes, each adapting the techniques and ideas we had shared with them. It was not to be.

However, surprisingly quickly after the pilot scheme entered the northern schools of Coventry in the Autumn of 1965, TIE became a national movement and a little later similar work opened up in Australia and the USA. And while more specific aims may be affected by local conditions I believe it to be generally true: the best of TIE sets out to provide positive learning experiences, whose very function explores problems (sometimes controversial), with integrity, challenging assumptions, encouraging creativity, thoughtfulness, empathy and imagination, and communicating something true about the human condition.

Post Script

The development of TIE from 1965–2015 was undoubtedly chequered yet, at the same time, it achieved a unique and outstanding body of work. It was possibly at its most active in the 1970s and 80s but once funding became difficult from 1988 with the Education Reform Act, TIE, in its original form as a free service, ceased to exist. Stuart Bennett explains as editor with great clarity in his introduction to *Theatre for Children and Young People* (Aurora Metro), the history and progress of TIE and other forms of theatre for and with young people.

This book is an optimistic reminder that creative and educationally purposeful theatre can exist in a variety of forms to delight, arouse questions and promote understanding. "Above all, " writes Bennett, "TIE was a form of empowering the participants' learning." It would be good to lose the past tense. His admirable, useful and stimulating record is now ten years old; the work of companies often goes in cycles, some disappear, others come into existence and it would be good to think another survey is underway, or if not a new one, perhaps an updating.

End Note

We live in challenging times, more intense now than ever before. Technology can become personally alienating as well as enriching opportunities, especially in communication; in 2015 there is however the overhanging threat of climate change; there is also the sharing of spaces and lifestyles with others of different cultural backgrounds in an increasingly overpopulated world, all in need of processes of education to encourage understanding and a mutual sense of well-being. Fifty years ago, because of the threat of a nuclear war, many young marrieds wondered whether it would be wise to bring children into the world. Children continued, and still continue to be born. Looking back I'm reminded that nothing remains static. What should be foremost in our minds is what kind of world we wish children to inherit – not just our children, but all children. There is a continuing need for TIE.

Notes

1. David Turner (1927–1990), author of a number of original plays for theatre and television, plus adaptations including Zola's *Germinal* and Sartre's *Roads to Freedom*. His most highly regarded play is *Semi-Detached*, which premiered at the Belgrade in 1963. For the Belgrade's seventh birthday celebrations he wrote a documentary drama, *Bottomley* – the true story of Horatio Bottomley who through his magazine *John Bull* and recruiting drives in World War I conned thousands of pounds out of working class investors.

2. Over the two years at the Belgrade I did get the chance to direct a couple of shows: the first was a devised piece about the life of Oscar Wilde to accompany a production of *The Importance of Being Earnest* and the second was a musical adaptation of *Maria Marten* or *Murder in the Red Barn*. I also had responsibility for the very first Belgrade Youth Theatre show, *Out of the Ashes*, with material written by Coventry writer, Nevil Malin, for the Belgrade's seventh birthday celebrations. This was followed later in 1965 by *Ars Longa Vita Brevis* by John Arden and Margaretta D'Arcy.

3. My own background seemed only partially appropriate for the demands of the post: I had spent eight years as an apprentice and journeyman in the printing industry; two years teacher training; two years as a secondary school teacher, specialising in Geography and English; did the school play and was bowled over by the children's response, and became aware of theatre as an educational transformative tool; met Brian Way who became a valued mentor; awarded a student/lectureship and did a year's specialist training in drama, followed by temporary teaching in London; did three productions with a North London Theatre Club; became a tutor for the then British Drama League and it was during that association that it was suggested I made contact with the Belgrade Theatre.

4. Sources referred to while writing memorandum:

Education Through Art, Herbert Read, (Faber and Faber), 1943, later republished by Random House, 1976.

Reflections, S. Clements, J. Dixon, L. Stratta, (Oxford University Press), 1963.

Child Drama, Peter Slade, (University of London Press), 1954.

Declaration, L. Andersen, K. Tynan, J. Osborne, D. Lessing, J. Wain etc., (MacGibbon and Kee), 1958.

Brecht on Theatre, John Willett, (Methuen), 1964.

Comprehensive Education, Robin Pedley, (Gollancz), 1956.

Listening and Writing, BBC; Film Education/BFI.

5. Brian Way (1923–2006) Artistic Director of Theatre Centre from 1953–1977. The theatre education movement, especially TIE, is indebted to Brian's pioneer work and inspirational spirit. He believed that; "theatre worked more deeply when actor and audience shared the same room, the same physical and psychological space, thus providing a more intuitive experience, stretching horizons and discovering greater truths…"

THE 'INCREDIBLE VANISHING' PLAYS

Our selection is built from the memories of people working today in the field of professional Theatre for Young Audiences in England. These are the plays which inspired them, challenged them, made them want to create theatre for young people.

There are many more plays which either appeared earlier than today's working artists remember or were highly successful for a time, for their times, or suited the taste of publishers. One could also make a (relatively short) list of the plays which have had most productions in the UK, or around the world – not necessarily the same. The many plays by Mike Kenny, Charles Way, Neil Duffield, David Wood and Alan Ayckbourn are widely known. Roy Kift's *Stronger than Superman* (1980) had only a couple of productions in the UK but has since been translated into 21 languages. The latest production was in Calcutta in 2014. This may well track the progress of public acceptability of the play's theme – disability.

We have picked from our shelves some published titles by writers our colleagues did not mention but who should not go unacknowledged. One such author – a theatre-maker and comic genius no longer with us – is Ken Campbell.

Ken translated Friedrich Waechter's *School for Clowns* (Unicorn Theatre, 1976) which was popular all over Europe but did not fit the more realistic, committed theatre of those most influenced by TIE practice. That did not stop Nottingham Playhouse Roundabout Company from commissioning Ken to write and direct *Skungpoomery* in 1975 and the cast was studded with actors who went on to lead important companies within the TIE movement. His *Old King Cole* was very popular as a Christmas show in regional theatres.

Alfred Bradley was a renowned BBC producer and playwright. His adaptations were commissioned by major regional theatres in the 70s and were staples of the holiday season repertoire, including *The Tale of the Red Dragon* for Octagon, Bolton in 1970, *Scatterbrained Scarecrow of Oz* for Chesterfield in 1971 and *Adventures of a Bear Called Paddington* for Nottingham Playhouse in 1973.

Adrian Mitchell, poet and dramatist, is perhaps most famous for Peter Brook's 1966 Vietnam War play *US*. But he wrote many plays for Unicorn Theatre, including *The White Deer* (1978) and *Wild Animal Song Contest* (1993). His adaptations of *The Lion, The Witch And The Wardrobe* and *Alice In Wonderland and Through The Looking Glass* were performed by the RSC in London and Stratford.

There are very good plays that may for many reasons have their moment of favour, fade, perhaps to return when the times require. We should record them while we can.

Here are a few: James Bridie: *Tobias and the Angel* (Festival Theatre, Cambridge, 1930)

Robert Bolt: *The Thwarting of Baron Bollingrew* (RSC, 1964)

Denise Coffey: *The Incredible Vanishing* (Young Vic, 1973)

Ken Campbell: *Old King Cole* (Victoria Theatre Stoke-on-Trent, 1967) *Skungpoomery:* (Nottingham Roundabout, 1975)

Peter Flannery and Mick Ford: *Adventures of Awful Knawful* (RSC, 1978)

Shaun Prendergast: *Little Victories* (Quicksilver & Trestle, 1994)

Philip Ridley: *Fairytaleheart* (Hampstead Theatre, 1998)

Abi Bown: *Hey There, Boy With The Bebop* (Polka, 2004)

Leeds TIE: *Flags and Bandages* (Leeds TIE, 1987)

The next few pages are examples of plays current in the early years as TIE companies became established and before TIE productions became recorded in the form of play texts.

1951

PINOCCHIO

by Brian Way and Warren Jenkins

Synopsis: A version of *The Adventures of Pinocchio* (1883), by the Italian writer Carlo Collodi. Carved by a woodcarver named Geppetto in a small Italian village, he was created as a wooden puppet but dreamed of becoming a real boy.

"This Pinocchio is the simple real 'it's ME' that every child will recognise, from his earliest attempts at living and walking, through his troubles, to the end. This play shows each living member of the audience a simple consideration of life itself, and makes possible a healthy and proper participation by all the little Pinocchios in that place; be they birds, beasts or just friends, they are by now all part of Pinocchio."

Peter Slade's Foreword to the script, 1953.

One of the most popular children's plays in Great Britain, professionally toured throughout Scandinavia, and the subject of broad-based critical acclaim, this stimulating interpretation reaches out and captures youthful audiences with unprecedented spirit. The timeless story of the wooden puppet who must earn the right to fulfil his longing to be a real boy brilliantly conveys lessons of responsibility and respect for the feelings of others. A charmingly innocent, powerfully believable play.

Originally produced by: Arena Theatre Company, Llandudno 1951

Cast: 5F, 7M, plus minor roles, doubling possible

Playing time: 1 hour 30 minutes plus interval

Audience recommendation: 5 years+ family

Script available from: Theatre Centre, Alibris Books.

Nominated by: David Wood

1964

THE MIRRORMAN
by Brian Way

Synopsis: A toymaker has a doll-that-can-walk-and-talk. One day, his life is suddenly interrupted by his reflection, Mirrorman, who needs help and protection from a Witch who is determined to steal his Book of Spells.

It was written and directed by the author for presentation in Junior Schools and was toured throughout the British Isles for a year.

The characters of Toyman and Mirrorman first appeared in Brian Way's *The Storytellers* (1955), although no reference is made to this in *The Mirrorman* (reportedly, there was a reference in an early version, but the audience and actors found it confusing).

Originally produced by: Theatre Centre in 1964

Cast: 2M, 2F: Toyman; Mirrorman, his reflection; Beauty, a doll that can walk and talk; Witch

Playing time: 50 minutes

Audience recommendation: 5–8 years

Script available from: British Library

Nominated by: Paul Harman

Paul Harman writes: I remember seeing one of these Brian Way shows in the 1960s, with children sat on the floor of the hall, on gym mats and benches, on all four sides of a square playing area about five metres across. This simple acting area, with exits at all four corners so the actors can move behind or through the audience, seen or 'not seen', offers a wide range of possible theatrical relationships. At times the children were asked by the characters to advise them and sometimes to join in by, for example, blowing away the wicked Witch. I used many of the principles of Way's arena staging all my working life in TYA.

1964

THE TINGALARY BIRD

by Mary Melwood

Synopsis: Imagine, if you will, a birdcage made of string which suddenly ripples with the majestic music of an antique Irish harp as the Old Man strums it. Imagine that music lifting the Old Woman to dizzying heights as she flies giddily through the air. A few minutes later it is only a poor drab birdcage again, and the Old Woman scoffs at the suggestion that she flew.

"A classic among 'theatre of the avant-garde' pieces for young people, recognizing that youngsters would be quick – often quicker than adults – to accept and grasp an absurdist plot and be absorbed by haunting, unanswered questions and images on a stage where nothing is as it seems to be. Audiences are held enthralled by the power of the language, and actors find an exciting opportunity playing the intriguing roles."

Originally produced by: Unicorn Theatre
Cast: 2M, 2F
Playing time: 1 hour 20 minutes

1966

THE ROYAL PARDON
by John Arden

Synopsis: After years of war, peace is to be reached between England and France, sealed by the marriage of the English prince and the French princess.

A company of actors are to be sent from England to Paris, to perform at a theatrical gala in celebration of the union. Croke's band of performers are carrying with them an ex-soldier, Luke, on the run from the law.

Circumstances twist, turn and contrive to place the soldier on the stage, with his new found beloved, where he must ad lib a play of great ingenuity to appease royalty, and the law's claim upon him.

Originally produced by: Beaford Festival, Devon, in 1966 with actors such as Maureen Lipman and John Arden in the cast. Later staged at Unicorn Theatre

Cast/Roles: 12M, 5F

Playing time: 2 Acts

Script available from: Bloomsbury Publishing/Casarotto

1966

THE THWARTING OF BARON BOLLIGREW
by Robert Bolt

Synopsis: Sir Oblong Fitzoblong, a highly unlikely knight-errant is sent by his duke to fight the black dragon with red eyes which lives on the Bolligrew Island – ruled over by the bold bad Baron Bolligrew and his henchman, Squire Blackheart.

After making friends with Magpie and Badger, and defying the magician Moloch in a display of magic, we end with an exciting confrontation with the dragon and Baron Bolligrew's 'conversation'.

Originally produced by: Royal Shakespeare Company

Robert Bolt wrote *A Man For All Seasons, The Tiger and the Horse* and the screenplay for the prizewinning film *Lawrence of Arabia*. Reviewers at the time claimed: "It is certain to take its place among the great children's classics, whose hallmark it seems to be that adults are no less enthusiastic in their addiction than the children."

A MOVEMENT BEGINS...

Soon after the establishment of the Belgrade Theatre in Education Company in 1965 many more teams were set up. Among other towns and cities where TIE flourished were Lancaster, Norwich, Ipswich, Bolton, Wigan, Leeds, Rochdale, Billingham, York, Greenwich, Swindon, Sheffield, Nottingham, Newcastle, Hull, Watford, Ellesmere Port...

Very few scripts have survived from the earliest years of Theatre in Education. Most of the work we created was devised collectively and recorded only in notes now in University archives.

Site-specific, participatory events in Roman forts, mediaeval halls or historic industrial sites were popular. A project about Gypsies and Travellers might use a caravan parked in the school grounds. An alien space ship could be discovered in the school hall. Many of these early 'programmes' involved meeting strange people and going on an imaginary journey with them, learning about their lives. More drama than theatre, perhaps, except that the actor/teachers were characters in role and the story line and some key moments, events, conflicts or expository conversations had been rehearsed and responses prepared for a range of interventions by the young participants.

Belgrade TIE created *Pow Wow* in which young children met a Native American – then of course called a 'Red Indian' – sitting in a cage in the school hall. Their decision about what to do with him was the point of the encounter, not a cultural performance or a historical lecture. Small numbers and intimate relations were essential for a quality experience and that had implications for cost and reach which influenced later policy changes. The more formal shows which we performed at Christmas were usually traditional pantomimes or adaptations.

Finally, in the early 1970s more scripted work began to emerge from permanent ensembles around the country. A movement had begun.

THE 50 BEST PLAYS SELECTION

VICKY IRELAND

It's been a great joy to compile fifty plays all chosen and nominated by TYA practitioners to celebrate a brilliant tradition of English playwriting for children and young people over the last fifty years.

All these plays have touched audiences' hearts, and they cover a tremendously wide spectrum, from joyful plays for little children to challenging plays for teenagers. You may wonder why there is more than one play by the same author. This is because the most popular writers were often attached to a TIE company for some years in the 1970s which offered a unique apprenticeship and the chance to learn their craft in collaborative teams, first as the one who wrote down the results of improvisations, then as shaper of the final text and finally as an author working to a commission and a content brief. Fully fledged, this resulted in numerous commissions for these writers and a string of first class plays resulted.

We also acknowledge the lack of female writers but that's historical fact and we can't change it.

So, here's our list and whilst the new is always exciting and challenging, let's also acknowledge and treasure gems from the past. We hope you discover many in this selection.

With our thanks to all those who wrote the plays, nominated the plays and wrote the citations.

1973 DRINK THE MERCURY by David Holman

1976 THE GINGERBREAD MAN by David Wood

1977 NO PARASAN by David Holman

1978 OPERATION ELVIS by C.P. Taylor

1979 TOWN MOUSE AND COUNTRY MOUSE
by Vicky Ireland

1980 STRONGER THAN SUPERMAN by Roy Kift

1981 BLOOD BROTHERS by Willy Russell

1981 CHAIRPERSON by Geoff Bullen

1982 PEACEMAKER by David Holman

1983 UNDER EXPOSURE by Lisa Evans

1984 NO WORRIES by David Holman

1984 RAJ
by Leeds Playhouse Theatre in Education Company

1985 GETTING THROUGH
by Nona Shepphard and Bryony Lavery

1987 WHISPERS IN THE DARK by Noël Grieg

1986 SHOUTING, STAMPING AND SINGING HOME
by Lisa Evans

1988 BAG DANCING by Mike Kenny

1988 ROSIE BLITZ by Richard Pinner

1989 INVISIBLE FRIENDS by Alan Ayckbourn

1990 THE FLOOD by Charles Way

1992 DREAMS OF ANNE FRANK by Bernard Kops

1994 THE BOMB by Kevin Dyer

1994 BRETEVSKI STREET by Lin Coghlan

1994 HOOD IN THE WOOD by Noël Grieg

1995 HOW HIGH IS UP? by Brendan Murray

1995 A SPELL OF COLD WEATHER by Charles Way

1995 INTO THE WEST by Greg Banks

1996 STEPPING STONES by Mike Kenny

1998 PLAYING FROM THE HEART by Charles Way

1998 THE BOY WHO FELL INTO A BOOK
by Alan Ayckbourn

1999 UNDER THE APPLE TREE
by Dave Tarkenter, Paul Harman and Philip Harrison

2000 SOULS by Roy Williams

2000 WALKING THE TIGHTROPE by Mike Kenny

2001 TALKING WITH ANGELS by Neil Duffield

2001 BREATHING SPACE by Mary Cooper

2001 RED RED SHOES by Charles Way

2001 WARRIOR SQUARE by Nick Wood

2001 HANNAH AND HANNA by John Retallack

2001 MY LONG JOURNEY HOME
    devised by NIE Company

2001 JUMPING ON MY SHADOW by Peter Rumney

2002 DIARY OF AN ACTION MAN by Mike Kenny

2003 SHOPPING FOR SHOES by Tim Crouch

2004 THE GARDENER by Mike Kenny

2005 BLUE by Tim Webb

2006 THE MONSTER UNDER THE BED by Kevin Dyer

2009 COSMOS by Peter Rumney

2011 CINDERELLA
    by Sally Cookson, Adam Peck and the Company

2013 TREE CHILD by Joseph Coelho

2013 WHOLE by Philip Osment

2014 MUCKY PUP by Daniel Jamieson

2015 HIDDEN by Kevin Dyer

1973

DRINK THE MERCURY
by David Holman

Synopsis: Loka is nine years old, the daughter of a fishing family in the Japanese coastal town of Minamata. It was the alarming behaviour of the cats feeding off fish scraps at the harbour that gave the first indication that something was wrong. Suddenly the cats would throw themselves about in a mad dance and then fall dead. Next it was the old people and the children who started to fall ill. Nobody knew at that time that a local factory was discharging effluent (including mercury) directly into the fishing grounds. Loka's story is told in mime, music, elements of kabuki theatre, and includes the verbatim words of the survivors.

The play is a response to the real-life Loka's dying wish – which was to sail in a small boat telling the world how she got the 'Minamata disease.' The campaign which her grieving parents mounted was to honour her memory and to fight what they came to call the Minamata war, the war against industrial pollution. The play has been produced in every continent.

Originally produced by: Belgrade Theatre in Education Company, Coventry

Cast: 2F, 2M

Playing time: 1 hour 10 minutes including interval

Audience recommendation: 8–12 years

Script available from: info@theagency.co.uk or david.holman3@btinternet.com

Nominated by: Nick Millington, David Johnston, David Wood

David Johnston writes: *Drink the Mercury* is an extraordinary and seminal piece of Theatre in Education.

Part of the *Rare Earth* trilogy, it was created by the excellent, second-phase Coventry Belgrade TIE company, which included superb actors, such as Sue Johnston, Maggie Steed and Clive Russell, with director David Pammenter.

Written by David Holman, in my view the country's foremost writer of theatre for children and young people in the last fifty years, the play tells the true story of the Mercury poisoning of the Minamata in Japan by the Chisso factory and the villagers' decision to take direct action to the highest level.

Utilising highly challenging kabuki style, music, drumming, and costume, and integrating it with excellent social content, Belgrade TIE set a standard for work that was aesthetically superb, and politically powerful. It invited both young people, their teachers, and their communities, to take a stance!

The piece inspired many other companies to develop this form of work and to develop new aesthetics in style, design and acting. It was enormously influential! It has been performed all over the world, translated into different languages, and still has a vital message for our times and for the future.

Photo: Theatre Centre

1976

THE GINGERBREAD MAN
by David Wood

Synopsis: *The Gingerbread Man* is set on a kitchen dresser. While the 'Big Ones' are asleep plenty of action is taking place.

The cuckoo-clock cuckoo has lost his voice and might be threatened with the dustbin in the morning if he doesn't recover it. The efforts of the newly-baked Gingerbread Man, the salt cellar and the pepper mill to help him regain it involve them in confrontations with the Old Tea Bag on the top shelf. Danger also comes from a voracious mouse and from the efforts of the 'Big Ones' to destroy the vermin by poison. All is resolved by morning, with the unobservant 'Big Ones' none the wiser.

Script available from: Play and piano/vocal score are published by Samuel French Ltd.

Included in David Wood: Plays One (Methuen)

First Class UK Professional and Foreign Rights, Casarotto Ramsay Ltd.

UK Repertory and Amateur Rights, Samuel French Ltd.

US Stock and Amateur Rights, Samuel French Inc.

Adam Stafford writes: *The Gingerbread Man* is in my opinion a master class in theatre for young children. Over the years I have enjoyed reading, watching and even having the pleasure of performing in this show. Of all David Wood plays, it still has the greatest impact on me. Maybe this is because of its instantly recognisable domestic and at first appearance, seemingly confined setting, the top of a kitchen dresser. Then each of the instantly recognisable but fully rounded characters, who you love (even if it's love to hate, to begin with)! Then the excitement and very real drama of each new situation or problem that has to be overcome.

Written in 1976 (I was 10) when generally there was perhaps still a 'second division' attitude to children's theatre, it is actually Mr Wood's author's note that says so much about what was to come:

'...audience participation works best when it is motivated by genuine concern for the characters and their problems; and this concern is motivated by the cast's genuine concern for them'.

And on the final page, even the Old Bag finds happiness by escaping from herself and making new friends, what more could you want? Perfect!

Photo: Keith Holly

1977

NO PARASAN
by David Holman

Synopsis: The play follows the life of a young German Jewish schoolboy boxing champion, Jan Goldberg.

We first see him in 1932 when his ambition is to box for his country at the upcoming Olympics in his home town of Berlin. However by 1936 Nazism has extended its control over every aspect of German life, including the exclusion of Jews from participation in any and all sports. Fleeing to London to try to make a living from professional boxing, Jan is witness to the rise of English Nazism and the Blackshirt invasion of the Jewish East End.

Later Jan responds to a request from his family to return to Germany and is never heard from again. A close friend, an English soldier, waiting for his demob in Berlin in 1945, attempts to find out what might have happened to Jan. As Allied lawyers prepare for the trials at Nuremburg the soldier starts to learn about 'the final solution' and what is likely to have happened to his friend.

Originally produced by: Octagon Bolton Theatre in Education Company

Cast: 2F, 4M

Playing time: 1 hour 30 minutes including interval

Audience recommendation: 14 years+

Script available from: info@theagency.co.uk or david.holman3@btinternet.com

Nominated by: Robert West

Robert West writes: I first saw this play as a teenager. It made me be proud to be from East London, proud of my parents who fought against the Nazis, and galvanised me to support the Anti-Nazi League which was so important in the late 70s.

The National Front very nearly won a Parliamentary seat in Shoreditch around that time and the East End needed to stand up again. This play is more than a period piece though. It's about resistance and making a stand. That's timeless and that's why this play should be included. It's inspiring, it's uplifting, and it's about making a change.

1978

OPERATION ELVIS
by C.P. Taylor

Operation Elvis was filmed for the BBC in 1980 and recorded for radio in 1982. It has since become a TYA classic, revived regularly by groups as varied as TAG, M6, Bruvvers, Northumberland Theatre Company, Tricycle Theatre and the Royal Shakespeare Company.

Synopsis: Ten-year-old Malcolm believes he is the reincarnation of Elvis Presley, but his mother and teachers are becoming frustrated with his fantasies. He runs away from his Newcastle home, heading for Memphis, Tennessee, but only gets as far as Morpeth, twenty miles away. There he meets Michael, a boy with extensive brain damage.

Malcolm and Michael become fast friends, despite Michael's inability to speak. Malcolm realises that his friend is desperate to go out on the local lake, but getting him into a boat seems impossible. With the help of Jackie, a local pigeon fancier, and Michael's carer Lynn, he constructs a harness to lift Michael safely from his wheelchair. The play closes with the two boys sailing blissfully across the water.

Originally produced by: Live Theatre Company, Newcastle upon Tyne

Cast: 3M, 1F

Playing time: 1 hour 5 minutes

Audience recommendation: 7–15 years

Script available from: www.alanbrodie.com

Nominated by: Ben Fletcher-Watson

1979

TOWN MOUSE AND COUNTRY MOUSE
by Vicky Ireland

Nominated as the ASSITEJ UK production for the ASSITEJ World Congress, New Orleans 2004. Subsequently produced at Polka Theatre, London, in the USA, South Africa, Australia and New Zealand.

Synopsis: William Boot, a country mouse, bored with country life in his grandmother's home, a hobnail boot called Toecap Cottage, is visited by his city cousin, Monty, and learns that he has inherited Tally-ho Lodge, a large hunting boot in London.

Joyfully, William departs with Monty and runs a gauntlet of adventures – among them a dangerous cat, poisons, traps, and the wiles of two tricky twin mice, Snowey and naughty Silver. An assured success for young audiences when imaginatively staged using the ingenious story book setting described in the text.

Originally produced by: Merseyside Young People's Theatre

Cast: 3F, 2M

Playing time: 1 hour 20 minutes plus interval

Audience recommendation: 6 years+

Script available from: www.anchoragepress.com

UK productions: vicky.ireland@virgin.net

Nominated by: Paul Harman, Roman Stefanski, Stephen Midlane

Roman Stefanski writes: I would like to say how much I enjoy Vicky Ireland's adaptation of *Town Mouse and Country Mouse* and endorse this play. I have directed this play twice, once at Polka Theatre and then again to packed houses on a national tour. Vicky has written an entertaining, good and simple story-line and has added the fun idea of: "a giant book set" as the main scenery, along with giant and animated 'turning' pages to visually help place the story's journey making it come alive.

The cast is made up of charming animal characters that engage in a dramatic quest and enjoy a fun adventure, with strong emotions and a little moral tale tucked in. It is a successful piece of writing for its age range and has received delightful reviews.

I personally love the world of "large props" in this show, which support the cast playing in their small skirting-board-world, magnified for our young audiences to enjoy. The scene showing a huge cat's head peering from above the book ingeniously depicts an enormous cat trying to capture the Country Mouse, along with a flailing long tail and one huge flexible paw extending from either side of the book, the whole spectacle teasing the children with screams of delight.

The philanthropist Dame Vivienne Duffield visited the show and couldn't believe that the reactions of the children weren't rehearsed, as they were so in tune with the action. The large button shield and darning needle sword from the production were gifted to Dame Vivienne and to this day still hang in her office.

Photo: Polka Theatre

1980

STRONGER THAN SUPERMAN
by Roy Kift

Synopsis: Chris, a boy of about ten, is confined to a wheelchair as a result of a birth defect called spina bifida ('split spine'). He has moved home with his sister and single mother and is confronted with misunderstanding and prejudice from the outside world.

The play is a comedy because it reverses audience expectations in a classical manner. Here the 'handicapped' family are stronger and more clever than the 'blind', 'deaf' and 'dumb' (both speechless and stupid) representatives of the so-called 'normal, healthy' outside world, whose prejudiced attitudes are exposed in their confrontation with Chris and his family. These include another schoolboy, Kevin, whose initial prejudices eventually turn into reluctant acceptance and then friendship. The family's struggles with the outside world, in the form of the man-made environment (transport, shops, entertainment facilities etc) and people themselves, here in the form of a security guard on an empty patch of building land, a social worker, a cinema owner, and the local education authority.

The play demonstrates how 'strong' so-called handicapped people need to be to be able to assert themselves and their rights in contemporary society. Hence it is an appeal to put aside prejudices of all sorts (Chris is, himself, prejudiced against girls and old people) and a plea for the integration of handicapped people, not only in schools, but into everyday life.

Originally produced by: Grips Theater, Berlin. 1980 (*Stärker als Superman*). English language premiere: Unicorn Theatre London 1981. It has since been continually produced all over the world from Iceland to New Zealand, and translated into 24 languages. The last recorded productions were in Bengali (Kolkata) and Korean (Seoul) in 2014/15.

Cast: 2F, 4M

Playing time: 1 hour 30 minutes plus interval.

Audience recommendation: 8–15 years

Script available from: Amber Lane Press.
www.amberlanepress.co.uk

Nominated by: Paul Harman

Paul Harman writes: The energetic, cabaret style of Grips was a challenge to the more realistic style of UK writing at the time. It was attractive, light-hearted and empowering. Roy Kift had absorbed the Grips ethos and perfectly caught the right tone to make playing with calipers and wheelchairs fun with a twist.

"If anyone believes it is impossible to talk about the problems of the handicapped (which are simultaneously the problems of the non-handicapped) in an entertaining and enlightening way … then I recommend a visit to the Grips Theater where you can learn a thing or two and also – who ever would have believed it! – have a good laugh."

Stuttgarter Nachrichten.

1981

BLOOD BROTHERS
by Willy Russell

Laurence Olivier Award for Best New Musical in 1983.

Synopsis: Twins separated at birth and brought up in a poor and a rich household meet as children but do not discover the truth about their relationship until much later. The play tells the story of their predestined lives and ends, as in a traditional ballad, in tragedy.

Originally produced by: Merseyside Young People's Theatre

Cast: 2M, 2F plus narrator M/F

Playing time: 1 hour 10 minutes

Audience recommendation: 14 years+

Script available from: Casarotto Ramsay and Associates

Nominated by: Paul Harman, Vicky Ireland

Paul Harman writes: Willy and I had adjacent rooms in the run-down house in Hope St, Liverpool, where the Everyman Theatre had its offices. He had a kettle and a commission inevitably followed, although I had to wait. After the RSC got a two-hander (*Educating Rita*) I got an epic musical, scaled down for touring to secondary schools and with only one song. For some years MYPT's version was in print for reading in schools. That it became one of the most long-lasting UK musicals, still touring thirty years later, is surely because Willy Russell found a deeper, mythical dimension in his simple story.

Played in the round with minimal props the show could move very fast. Each short scene is intense and stripped to essentials but full of humour and humanity. For a group of talented young actors it is a joy to perform. Our audiences were gripped by it. Best of all, perhaps, is that this version could be packed into a small van and played twice a day in different secondary schools with no technical paraphernalia, just live actors right there.

1981

CHAIRPERSON
by Geoff Bullen

Synopsis: Dudley, an intelligent and cheerful 14 year old, is confined to a wheelchair. He attends a special school for the disabled, spending the holidays at home. As the summer vacation draws to an end, however, he refuses to return, pleading his right to a 'normal' education at the nearby comprehensive.

Trouble! The local school is 'not designed for wheelies'. Will he be accepted by the other children? More importantly, must father and sister make even more sacrifices to care for him full-time? Dudley's determination to be treated fairly throws everything into confusion. But, at the last moment all is resolved happily enough as Dudley himself makes the first moves towards his goal.

Originally produced by: Theatre Centre

Cast: 1F, 2M

Playing time: 50 minutes

Audience recommendation: 9–13 years

Script available from: Theatre Centre <u>admin@theatre-centre.co.uk</u>

Nominated by: David Johnston

David Johnston writes: In 1980 Theatre Centre decided to devote a year to the theme of disability. This was at a time when Graeae were still struggling for recognition and funding disabled theatre was not encouraged.

As a company dedicated to supporting social change we felt we should support the disability movement. Our way of doing it was to create two projects about disability, to inform young people, teachers and families. In *Wheels*, for 5–8 year-olds, we worked with blind athlete Graeme Salmon to explore the potential of blind running.

For older children we created *Chairperson*, written by Geoff Bullen in collaboration with the acting team. This piece looked at the situation of a young boy with cerebral palsy, who wanted to move from a special school to mainstream, explored the family consequences, his relationship with others and especially his desires, passion and commitment. It also asked the audience for solutions.

It has been presented many times with disabled actors and its effect on our mainstream work was massive!

1982

PEACEMAKER
by David Holman

This play has been produced all over the world.

Synopsis: In a small way, the play raises the subject of racism for a very young audience. Long ago the Reds and the Blues lived together harmoniously. Then (though nobody quite remembers how any more) a schism occurred so serious that a wall had to be constructed across the country. The Reds have been living ever since then on one side and the Blues on the other.

Myths proliferate on both sides of the wall about the 'other' and, to this day, no Blue has ever met a Red, nor vice versa. But today they will. A Red youngster, Simp, has been ordered to perform some juggling at a big Red Carnival the following day – but therein lies a small problem – she can't juggle. So Simp ignores the dusk-time klaxon rung to keep everyone away from the wall. It's the only place where she can practice without being observed…

Originally produced by: Theatre Centre
Cast: 2M, 2F
Audience recommendation: 5–7 years
Playing time: 45 minutes
Script available from: david.holman3@btinternet.com
Nominated by: Janys Chambers, Tony Graham, Dot Wood, Robert West, Geoff Readman

Geoff Readman writes: *Peacemaker* is a most poignant and moving text for young audiences. It is a wonderful example of the value of theatre that is specifically written and designed for children. The play engages and entertains whilst, at the same time, prompting sensitive considerations of dilemmas and issues that emerge from a fictional fable. It explores how co-operation, friendship and direct, playful communication will resolve conflict situations.

In the 80s, I witnessed several productions of *Peacemaker* by Theatre Centre and Nottingham Roundabout. They enabled young children to grapple with such concepts as friendship, war, prejudice and peace.

In 2015, I had the privilege of directing *Peacemaker* in Chengdu, China. It was an unforgettable experience, but the ending of the play served to remind me of its universal dilemma; the children of the Blues and Reds cannot resolve the problems their ancestors have created and the wall between them must remain in place.

Paul Harman writes: It is a tiny footnote in the history of TIE and TYA in the UK that around the time this play was written many serious theatre-makers re-discovered circus and our very British variety theatre tradition, of pantomime and physical skills in dance, acrobatics and juggling. To this day, many of us can still keep three balls in the air for a few seconds. But it was also an important lesson to be learned that it requires both talent *and* a lifetime's dedication to become a juggler worth watching.

Photo: Theatre Centre

1983

UNDER EXPOSURE
by Lisa Evans

Winner British Theatre Association Best Play For Young People 1986.

Synopsis: A white sports photographer visits Cape Town, South Africa and meets a family living in Crossroads Squatter camp. Using songs and stories we learn of their lives under apartheid.

Originally produced by: Theatre Centre

Cast: 4F [3 black, 1 white]

Playing time: 1 hour

Audience recommendation: 8 years+

Script available from: diana@mbalit.co.uk

Nominated by: Phil Clarke, Angela McSherry

Phil Clarke writes: *Under Exposure* heralded a landmark change in the TIE/YPT movement. The product of an all-women's production company within Theatre Centre, London, the original production had a predominantly black cast and was a celebratory result of positive discrimination within the creative process. Above all it remains a well-crafted, beautifully written play that promotes internationalism within a young person's learning and never fails to touch and disturb its audience.

NO WORRIES
by David Holman

Winner 1986 Australian Writers Guild, AWGIE Award for Best Children's Drama.

Synopsis: The writing of *No Worries* was a response to two simultaneous events in Australia, both of which had a profound effect on children. The first was the worsening of a year's long outback drought and the second, the arrival on the Continent's northern shores of Vietnamese refugee families fleeing their war-devastated country – these were 'the boat people.'

The two central characters are the farm girl Matilda, and refugee Binh. Matilda's family, having survived the drought for years, are finally forced off the land as their sheep starve and are, in any event, valueless. Matilda will not accept her new life in the hated city and retreats into silence. Binh finds herself in the same city where the walls are daubed with the message 'Boat People go Home.' What hope is there for either of them?

Originally produced by: Magpie Theatre (young people's arm of the State Theatre of South Australia).

Cast: 3M, 3F actor/musicians

Playing time: 1 hour 50 minutes including interval

Audience recommendation: 8 years+

Script available from: info@theagency.co.uk

Published in 'Three Plays for Children' by David Holman, Currency Press, Sydney, Australia, 1989. Subsequently produced in London, Birmingham, Manchester, Chicago, Tel Aviv and Tokyo

Nominated by: Vicky Ireland, Kumiko Mendl

Kumiko Mendl writes: it was my good fortune to be cast as Binh in *No Worries* by David Holman in a wonderful production at Polka Theatre directed by Roman Stefanski.

We had a great cast that bonded instantly and I remember having such an enjoyable time rehearsing and learning and singing all the songs.

It's a beautifully crafted and moving piece. Holman really knows what resonates with a child with great songs and humour and inclusion of lots of animals! He tells a very touching and true story of a young girl finding her voice again through a gradual flowering of friendship. A situation that must be happening all over the world right now, but not always with a happy ending.

There are precious few parts written specifically for East Asian characters and few stories that mention the Vietnam War and its effects. I also gained my Equity card performing in Holman's *Small Poppies* so I am doubly grateful to David for bringing to light these important stories for young audiences in such a sensitive and universal way.

1984

RAJ

by Leeds Playhouse Theatre in Education Company

Synopsis: *RAJ* is set in India during British administration. It is a play about imperialism, about power and where it lies, about divided loyalties: loyalties born, nurtured and handed down over generations of British rule. The Indian characters are not victims. They are people who believed that the British represented 'fair play, tolerance, decency and equality'. Forced to face the realities of British rule in India, they struggle to make sense of their personal relationships with the British in the face of violence towards their own people.

RAJ was originally devised, researched and performed by the eight members of Leeds Playhouse Theatre in Education Company.

Originally produced by: Leeds TIE
Cast: N/A
Playing time: 1 hour
Audience recommendation: 12+
Script available from: Amber Lane Press
Nominated by: Peter Rumney, Lawrence Evans, Richard Pinner, Phil Clarke

Paul Harman writes: Suddenly our expectations of TIE rose into a new league. We came of age, perhaps, twenty years after those early, worthy, participatory events closer to drama lessons than theatre that we started out with in Coventry. This was a proper play with mature performers who also cared passionately about politics and history. It was as near as we ever came to the fully realised, collectively created, unique style which characterises the best independent touring companies in Europe and UK. Its creation required a permanent ensemble with time and a freedom to experiment rarely found today.

1985

GETTING THROUGH
by Nona Shepphard and Bryony Lavery

Synopsis: Caz is a girl who is different, who prefers to wear trousers and build radio transmitters in a world where girls wear skirts to school and sigh over the colour pink and pop stars.

She is befriended by two kindred spirits – Lady Cleaner and Silk Willoughby; but when her best friend Boy moves away, she is desperate and broadcasts to the world in the final song, *Is There Anyone Out There?*

Getting Through is a musical, part of a project which developed in conjunction with two writers and directors, Nona Shepphard and Bryony Lavery in autumn 1985.

Originally produced by: Theatre Centre
Cast: 4F + 1 musician
Playing time: 1 hour
Audience recommendation: 9–13 years
Script available from: admin@theatre-centre.co.uk
Nominated by: Janys Chambers, David Johnston

Janys Chambers writes: I've nominated *Getting Through* as much for its context as for the play itself. It toured during the heyday of young people's theatre – when it was properly-funded and prolific. The producing company, Theatre Centre, was full of extraordinary talents (like the wonderful writers Bryony Lavery and Noël Greig, and designer Bill Mitchell, later to run Kneehigh and Wildworks.) The original cast wasn't bad either. (But I'm biased. I was in it.)

Getting Through was innovative as a specially-commissioned musical that tackled gender stereotyping through story, comedy, pathos, and song, and which was performed by a 'Women's Company' – an all-female unit within Theatre Centre. (There was a 'Mixed Company' too – diverse in gender, ethnicity and sexual orientation. Theatre Centre was in the vanguard by many years of the Arts Council's 'creative case for diversity'.)

The play tells the story of Caz, who likes wearing trousers and building radios and whose best friend is a sensitive younger boy. Going up to 'big school' Caz finds her individuality mocked and almost crushed by her peers.

It's still relevant.

Getting Through was fun to perform and hugely successful, touring London schools and YPT Festivals in Canada and the US.

1987

WHISPERS IN THE DARK
by Noël Grieg

Synopsis: Once upon a time, everyone in the land was happy, telling stories and singing songs, keeping our history alive. Then the giants came…

The play was originally written for a mixed-race cast and wherever possible this integrated casting should be retained. The two performers playing Alf and Beth were on that occasion young black women and although to have these characters played by performers of different race would not rob the play of meaning, this casting does add a layer of meaning which the author regarded as particularly important. In the original production this was underlined by the fact that Beth (the woman who has been robbed of her memory by the giants) had white make-up smeared on her. When she came to recognise her sister and herself, she wiped this away, providing a very strong and moving image for the audience as she came to accept and understand what had happened to her.

Originally produced by: Theatre Centre Young People's Theatre

Cast: 2M, 2F

Playing time: 50 minutes

Audience recommendation: 5–8 years

Original songs by Shaz Nassauer

Script available from: www.alanbrodie.com and the Noël Greig Archive c/o Rose Bruford College theatrefutures.org. uk/noel-greig-script-catalogue/

Nominated by: Tony Graham

Tong Graham writes: Once upon a time, everyone in the land was happy, telling stories and singing songs, keeping our history alive. Then the giants came…

Three storytellers on the run, a long-lost sibling, menacing giants: these are the ingredients in Theatre Centre's much-loved, *Whispers in the Dark* by Noël Greig. Like Brian Friel's *Translations*, it was inspired by the rural Irish 'hedge schools' of the 18th and 19th centuries, in which local teachers fought to preserve Irish culture and language from colonial repression.

Ultimately this play is about the struggle to discover who, behind the mask, we really are. Theatre Centre's version featured a black actor with white face paint which was removed as the play reached its liberating climax. When I directed it for TAG Theatre, Glasgow, Noël suggested that the text be adapted into Scots by John Binnie. It has since been performed in Nigeria and Wales suggesting that the central metaphor in the play speaks to many cultures.

If it all sounds a bit worthy, don't worry: this mischievous play for younger audiences is swept along by Noël's love of story and poetry. Richly textured and moving, it deserves its place in the canon of theatre for young audiences.

Photo: Theatre Centre

1986

SHOUTING, STAMPING AND SINGING HOME
by Lisa Evans

Synopsis: The play was inspired by the life of Sojourner Truth, the well-known abolitionist and early feminist. It tells the story of her fictional great, great granddaughter, Lizzie Walker, and her transformation from child to adult activist in the southern states of America. Through the songs and stories of the women in her family, Lizzie comes to understand the importance of her own past and her place in history.

Originally produced by: Watford Palace Theatre in Education Company

Cast: 4 black women

Playing time: 1 hour

Audience recommendation: 10 years+

Script available from: www.oberonbooks.com

Nominated by: Brendan Murray, Vicky Ireland

Brendan Murray writes: I saw this play, I think, at an Arts Council conference at Warwick University in 1984 when I was working with the Belgrade TIE Company. We'd been trying ourselves to find forms – find a language – that would free our work from its potentially dry, issue-based origins and here it was: joyful, vibrant, complex.

A play for young people, certainly, but also one that could speak to adults without any sense of compromise.

I was blown away by its sheer theatricality and verve. It certainly showed a way forward and its continued success is no surprise. Not just an important play for young audiences. An important play.

1988

BAG DANCING
by Mike Kenny

Synopsis: *Bag Dancing* explores the touching relationship between Imelda, a bag lady, and Neville, a caretaker. Both are advanced in years and they develop a warm friendship. While one is forever going somewhere, the other has nowhere to go. Through their conversations we learn about their lives and experiences, their personal and social histories. "Their tales are both humorous and poignant, challenging many preconceptions about old age." – BBC

Originally produced by: Theatre Company Blah Blah Blah, Leeds

Cast: 1F, 1M

Playing time: 1 hour

Audience recommendation: All ages

Script available from: www.alanbrodie.com

Nominated by: Maria Hayes, Anthony Haddon

Maria Hayes writes: A chilly church hall surrounded by bags of jumble wasn't the most inspiring place to work, and yet out of this unpromising beginning came *Bag Dancing*. We worked with stories – real and imaginary – and we raided the jumble to help. A shoe became a phone, a suit was held as a dancing partner and a small jumper triggered a story about a lost child. We improvised with the remains of other people's stories from bags of jumble.

On the day we realized that we didn't need a designed set – that we could simply use two clothes rails and bin bags of jumble, I felt redundant. Hired as the designer, I suddenly had no place. However, I also realized that this decision was right for the integrity of the piece. When the final script was in and rehearsals began, the full richness of Mike Kenny's writing became apparent. I was also part of the team who devised and delivered workshops post-performance. Working in youth clubs and schools, we were able to take the piece in many directions, covering stories and experiences of war, alienation, secrecy and loss. The *Bag Dancing* workshops were some of the most moving work I have done in a thirty year career as artist facilitator.

1988

ROSIE BLITZ
by Richard Pinner

British Theatre & Drama Magazine Best Young Person's Play
1988.

Synopsis: The first act of the play is set in London's East
End during the Blitz, which had a devastating impact on that
part of the city at the beginning of World War II.

A child is rescued from a bombed and burning house by
a German Jewish immigrant, Willie Muller. And, suffering
from amnesia, Rosie is informally adopted by Willie and a
neighbour, Moma Waleski, where she finds love and security
in this poor émigré community. That is, until the authorities
catch up with her – in the shape of a WVS billeting officer,
Mrs. Dandridge – and Rosie is forcibly evacuated to the
country and apparent safety.

So, at the beginning of act two, Rosie finds herself in the
middle class home of Mrs. Dandridge, in the depths of rural
Northamptonshire, torn from the culture which has made her
so welcome. Here, except for her only friend, the maid Ivy,
she feels totally isolated and is picked on by the some of the
local children. She is even instructed, by Mrs. Dandridge, to
discontinue her correspondence with Willie, whose racial mix
makes him doubly undesirable. However the spirited Rosie
has other ideas about her destiny and, throwing caution to the
wind, makes her escape in an attempt to find her way back to
her beloved 'home'…

Originally produced by: Polka Theatre

Cast: 10 year old girl plus 2F, 2M doubling

Playing time: 1 hour 15 minutes, or 1 hour 35 minutes
with interval

Audience recommendation: 8 years+

Script available from: richard.pinner@btopenworld.com

Nominated by: Stephen Midlane

Stephen Midlane writes: Polka Theatre staged this play twice, in 1988 and again in 1995 (to mark the fiftieth anniversary of the ending of the Second World War).

It was a bold and thrilling production which shone a light on the extraordinary transformation that so many British children experienced at the time and vividly communicated the experience of war to its young audience.

Vicky Ireland adds: The two little girls who took turns to play the part of Rosie, Lucy Speed and Keeley Hawes, are now well established actresses.

Photo: Polka Theatre

1989

INVISIBLE FRIENDS
by Alan Ayckbourn

Synopsis: When Lucy's imaginary friend Zara becomes all too real and offers to make her family disappear, Lucy is all to happy to agree. But when Zara's much worse family appears in their place, Lucy has to deal with the consequences of her actions and find a way to bring her own family home.

Originally produced by: Stephen Joseph Theatre in The Round, Scarborough and subsequently at The National Theatre.

Cast: 3F, 4M

Playing time: 1 hour 40 minutes plus interval

Audience recommendation: 6 years+

Script available from:

Amateur: Details at www.samuelfrench-london.co.uk

Professional: Contact mel@casarotto.co.uk

Nominated by: Vicky Ireland

(See Steve Marmion's article on Alan Ayckbourn's writing for young audiences.)

1990

THE FLOOD
by Charles Way

Synopsis: *The Flood* is a modern re-telling of the biblical tale about Noah and his Ark. It was written for the Unicorn Theatre and has since had many productions. What marked out the original production was that the two children in the story were played by actors well into their 60s. It is unfortunate that with climate change the play has become ever more relevant.

An ordinary middle class family face another ordinary day, but it turns out to be a day like no other. Rain has begun to fall and will not stop. Martha, has had a dream and believes the end of the world is nigh, but her businessman husband Gerald thinks she is ill and needs to see a doctor. Their two children watch as the rain falls and their parents argue. Gerald refuses to believe Martha and goes to work while she blows their savings on a yellow boat. She orders the children to pack enough clothes and food for a long journey. Gerald reaches the boat just in time as the world is washed away – except it seems for one yellow boat. Eventually, after much hardship, the family reach an island which is a natural paradise, and the children begin to rebuild their lives and create a new culture. As the play ends, they see another ship on the horizon.

Originally produced by: Unicorn Theatre, London

Cast: 1M, 1F + 1M aged 6 years, 1F aged 11 years

Playing time: 1 hour 30 minutes including interval

Audience recommendation: 6–12 years

Script available from: Collins Educational ISBN 0-00-330304-7

Translated into Russian, Welsh and German: Theaterstückverlag München

Nominated by: Dot Wood, Paul Harman

Kevin Lewis writes: This was the first play I directed at Theatr Iolo and holds a very special place in my heart. I'd only been directing a short time and was excited to get my teeth into this wonderful re-imagination of the Noah story with its epic staging requirements – Martha's apocalyptic dream, an all engulfing flood, setting sail on a yacht, stuck in the middle of the ocean in a lifeboat and marooned on a desert island. All interesting and exciting challenges for a youngish director and the creative team I had assembled to try to solve.

And then there was the text itself with its mix of poetry, rich themes and examination of some of the big questions of life: How should we live with other people? What is the nature of the power relationships in a family group between male and female, between child and adult? What in life is truly of value?

Our young audience of 8–12 year-olds in school halls in South Wales were as gripped by it as we were, with one child summing it up by saying "This play treats us like we are grown-ups."

And I will always remember the stunned silence when on the lifeboat in the middle of the ocean Gerald, the father, makes his children throw their toys overboard whilst still clinging to his briefcase and when challenged by them says that it contains "important things"!

1992

DREAMS OF ANNE FRANK

by Bernard Kops

Winner London Fringe Award Best Children's Production 1992.

Joint Winner for Time Out award for Best Children's Production 1992.

Nominated for a Writer's Guild Award for Best Fringe Play 1992.

Synopsis: The play is set in war-time Amsterdam and is seen through the eyes of a teenager. Anne's Diary is the starting point. Dream logic and songs explore the inner and outer words of her world.

Originally produced by: Polka Theatre

Cast: 4F, 4M

Playing time: 1 hour 30 minutes with new and appropriate songs

Audience recommendation: 10 years+ and subsequently it has been produced and worked well for younger and older people.

Script available from: www.knighthallagency.com/

Methuen Student editions. Oberon Books. Samuel French Ltd.

Nominated by: Leni Hill, Stephen Midlane, Vicky Ireland

Leni Hill writes: Out of a time that was all about unimaginable fear and death, Bernard Kops created a play full of the deep human need for joy and survival in the midst of desperate circumstances. By his sensitive telling of the true story of one young girl growing to maturity in the confines of the Secret Annexe and her eventual betrayal to the Nazis, the horror of the Holocaust is made intimate and personal.

1994

THE BOMB
by Kevin Dyer

Synopsis: Based on the remarkable friendship between Jo Berry, whose father was killed in the Brighton bombing, and IRA-man Pat Magee, who made and planted the bomb. The Brighton bombing was called the boldest attack on the British government since the Gunpowder plot.

The play, in the background of a major political event, tells a personal story: when the bomb killed her father, Jo Berry knew that she would not let the hatred carry on inside her; instead she determined to find and meet whoever planted it. She did that – and the two (the Tory politician's daughter and the IRA bomber) have since become friends working together to bring about peace.

Originally produced by: Action Transport Theatre
Cast: 2F, 2M 4/5 actors minimum
Playing time: 1 hour 20 minutes
Audience recommendation: 12 years+
Script available from: info@aurorametro.com
Nominated by: Joe Sumsion

Joe Sumsion writes: I doubt I will ever forget the second week of rehearsals of *The Bomb*, when Jo Berry and Pat Magee came to talk to us and see an early rehearsal of the scene when they first met each other. 'Could you meet the man who killed your father?' was the strapline for the show, and here we were, with the woman who did, trying to tell a story of courage, politics and forgiveness. I'm delighted that Kevin's play has been included in this selection. It's a psychological thriller of sorts, made for anyone 14+ and originally written to tour into secondary schools and theatres. I think it's a bold, challenging play and a fitting reflection of the remarkable relationship which inspired it.

BRETEVSKI STREET
by Lin Coghlan

Synopsis: Cormac and Vas are best friends. They are both 11 and live next door to each other in Bretevski Street. Cormac lives with Isobel, his mother, and his grandmother, Hortense. Next door Pierre lives with his son Vas. Pierre is a free spirit, who has made his home in Bretevski Street but wasn't born there. He is a congenial neighbour and someone who would rather forget the past. He abhors the old stories of war and wants to focus on the future. Pierre is in love with Cormac's mother Isobel but is too shy to tell her. Two families living side by side, sharing food in their gardens as their two boys play together, best friends.

When war creeps ever closer to the town, divisions start to appear in the community, and Pierre and his son soon become the focus of prejudice and threats. Slowly, Cormac is drawn into the conflict and when he joins a brigade for child soldiers he starts to regard his friend with suspicion. As the town is surrounded and starvation takes hold, each family betrays the other, and the result is that one of the boys must leave on a bus, possibly never to return.

In a downward spiral of fear, self-preservation and prejudice, who is to blame when the children are parted forever?

Originally produced by: Theatre Centre
Cast: 2F, 3M
Playing time: 1 hour
Audience recommendation: 10–13 years
Script available from: www.unitedagents.co.uk
Nominated by: Stuart Bennett

Nick Wood writes: It's twenty past two on a Friday, and, still a teacher, I'm waiting in the school theatre for the students to file in for a performance by the Nottingham Playhouse Roundabout Company. Friday afternoon was all I could get when I booked them. Friday afternoons can be hard work. I needn't have worried. An hour and ten minutes later the bell for the end of school has gone and those who haven't a bus to catch are still sitting with the cast discussing the play they've just seen – Bretevski Street.

What got them so involved? The location was a world away from their ex pit village, still hurting and divided from the miners' strike, but they knew about families in crisis, friendships broken by pressures outside their control, what can happen when a community is forced into taking sides. But that wouldn't have been enough, on its own, to hold them. They were pulled in by characters, which were flawed, passionate, caring, unkind, human, and real; by writing that never patronised. They didn't go home with the bell because in challenging them the play had treated them as the thoughtful, mature people they were learning to become.

1994

HOOD IN THE WOOD
by Noël Greig

Synopsis: A retelling of the story of *Little Red Riding Hood*.

Originally produced by: Nottingham Playhouse Roundabout

Cast: 2F, 2F/M (4 in total)

Playing time: 1 hour

Audience recommendation: 8–12 years

Script available from: info@aurorametro.com

Published in *Tin Soldier and Other Plays for Children* (Aurora Metro) ISBN 978-1-906582-19-7

Nominated by: David Johnston, Jayne Williams, Sally Siner, Richard Pinner

David Johnston writes: Noël Greig (1944–2009) created a number of excellent plays for young people, mainly for Theatre Centre and Nottingham Playhouse Roundabout in the 80s and 90s, one of which was *Hood in the Wood*.

In 2003, when Ava Hunt, Gary Lagden and I decided to create a new company – Tangere Arts – to create innovative and minimalist work in Derbyshire, Noël was obviously the writer of choice. His new version of the traditional tale took the young people's theatre world by storm! We initially planned a small schools' tour, but were joined by our old comrade Lewis Gibson, as musician/MD, who helped to transform the piece when we presented the show around the East Midlands.

Owing to a positive intervention by Tony Graham, director of Unicorn Theatre, and his associate, Rosamunde Hutt, the play became a massive hit in London and then regionally and internationally. It is a poetic piece, utilising the Red Riding Hood story to tell an extraordinary 'rites of passage' tale, utilising physical theatre, music, and soundscape. Noël wrote two more shows for the company, *A Tasty Tale* and *Tin Soldier*, before his untimely passing in 2009: he is still much missed!

1995

HOW HIGH IS UP?

by Brendan Murray

The play has been produced many times in the UK and abroad.

Synopsis: Learning of the imminent death of her friend/guardian, Ba Gia, Little Star sets out on a quest to try and make time stand still. Accompanied by The Bird Who Has No Wings, she visits The Magicians of The Roaring Winds, Pouring Rains & Silent Snows before realising time will never stand still (nor should it) and that, painful as it may be, it is right that Ba Gia should die. Bereft, angry and afraid, she dances through her grief and finds strength to face the future.

Originally produced by: Theatre Centre

Cast: 4/5 flexible

Playing time: 45–60 minutes depending on the production.

Audience recommendation: Target audience: 5–8 years

Script available from: www.brendanmurray.co.uk

Nominated by: Tony Graham, Peter Rumney, Lawrence Evans

Lawrence Evans writes: The genius of this play is that Brendan has put the 'heart' of the child on stage in the character of Little Star, experiencing and feeling everything that happens as it happens. The children see themselves standing centre stage and identify with Little Star and exactly what she's going through; her joy, her pain, her loss, her sadness. They see through her eyes, they feel through her heart. On the first performance I sat in an audience of 4-year-olds and their teachers and was so deeply affected by the whole experience that it has stayed with me ever since. The teachers all cried, but the children did more, they empathised with Little Star and wanted to comfort her in her sadness. Unlike adults, under-5s have not yet learnt to put up barriers to sensing the world and emotionally connecting to the people they meet. Brendan's writing expands our understanding of childhood itself.

1995

A SPELL OF COLD WEATHER

by Charles Way

Winner of the Writer's Guild Award for Best Children's Play.

Synopsis: The play is set on a farm, which is the home of two down-in-the-mouth farmers, Betty and Bob. They have lost touch with each other, their animals and their own culture. In the time between Christmas and New Year, Betty and Bob get a surprise – their little niece Holly needs to come and stay because her Mum is having an operation. When Holly arrives she feels very alone, in a strange world with no friends.

Things pick up however when she meets Tomos Trickman – a puck-like fairy who explains to Holly how the two farmers have forgotten how to sing, dance and play games, and worst of all they refuse to believe he exists and have stopped putting food out for him in the traditional manner. Together, Holly and Tomos bring the farm back to spiritual health and the play ends with an unforgettable magical New Year's night party.

Originally produced by: Sherman Theatre, Cardiff and Theatre Centre.

Cast: 2F, 2M

Playing time: 1 hour

Audience recommendation: 4–8 years, their friends and families.

Script available from: info@aurorametro.com

Published by Aurora Metro ISBN 0954233085

A German translation is available from Theaterstückverlag München

Nominated by: Paul Harman

Rosamunde Hutt writes: Who would have thought a play about grumpy Welsh hill farmers, a mischievous faery and a girl from the city would reach so many corners of the earth? *A Spell of Cold Weather* ran for eight consecutive years in Cologne, has played in Ireland, America and Canada, and has been translated into Welsh, German, Norwegian, Greek, French and Serbian.

This is a magical tale, somehow both ancient and modern, suffused with poetry, humanity and an abundance of fun. We chose to revive it for Theatre Centre's 50th birthday – a perfect springboard into the future, a play about rebirth, about the importance of culture, about the need to be subversive and turn the world upside down, and featuring a resourceful little girl as the agent of change.

This is a play where the soul, personified by Tomos Trickman, is nourished not just by a plate of broad beans and a dollop of cream but by uplifting song and joyous dance and madcap games. Bringing warmth to the cold, joy to the heart, and love to a frozen world, it deserves its place amongst the finest children's plays of our era.

PRODUCTION IMAGES

Left:
*Walking The
Tightrope*
by
Mike Kenny

Photo:
Ted Giffords

Below:
*Dreams of
Anne Frank*
by
Bernard
Kops

Photo:
Polka Theatre

Left:
Rosie Blitz by
Richard Pinner

Photo:
Polka Theatre

How High is Up by Brendan Murray Photo: Simone Neumayr

PRODUCTION IMAGES

Right:
*The Town Mouse
and the
Country Mouse*
by Vicky
Ireland

Photo:
Polka Theatre

The Gardener by Mike Kenny Photo: Philip Carr

Above: *Hood in the Wood* by Noël Grieg Photo: University of Derby
Below: *The Bomb* by Kevin Dyer Photo: George Coupe

PRODUCTION IMAGES

Above: *Whispers in the Dark* by Noël Grieg
Photo: Theatre Centre

Below: *Into The West* by Greg Banks
Photo: Camilla Adams

INTO THE WEST
by Greg Banks

Samuel Beckett award for Best Children's Production, Dublin International Theatre Festival 1999.

Synopsis: Ally and Finn are Traveller children, whose mother has died and whose grief-stricken father has brought them to live in a tenement flat on the outskirts of Dublin. Here they are visited by their grandfather, who brings them a white horse which has first appeared on the seashore, and has followed him to the city. He tells them it is called Tir na n'Og, after the legendary land of eternal youth which lies under the sea off the West coast of Ireland.

The children take it up in the lift to their flat on the fourteenth floor. But the neighbours complain, and after one fierce dispute the police are called to get the horse out of the building. After a chase across the country the police close in on them and Tir na n'Og plunges into the waves. The children stare out to sea and realise at last it was the spirit of their dead mother, bringing them a message of hope and renewal.

"Not just exceptional children's theatre, it is complex, moving and vivid theatre that creates a complete imaginative world of its own and treats its young audience with a generous and quiet respect."

– The Guardian

Originally produced by: Travelling Light Theatre Co, Bristol, under the title *Tir na n'Og*

Cast: 2M, 1F + 1 musician

Playing time: 1 hour 10 minutes

Audience recommendation: 8 years+

Script available from: travellinglighttheatre.org.uk/

Nominated by: Dot Wood, Jude Merrill

Dot Wood writes: I was extremely fortunate to see a performance of *Tir na n'Og* at the 1995 Take Off festival and then again later with a family audience at The Brewery Arts Centre, Kendal.

It seems impossible to separate the play itself from the inspirational style of Travelling Light's production. The highly physical storytelling and evocative live music was breathtaking – transporting us on an exciting and deeply moving roller-coaster ride.

Tir na n'Og was skilfully and imaginatively adapted by Greg Banks from Jim Sheridan's screenplay for the 1992 film – *Into the West*.

It has a beautiful multi-layered quality, mixing Irish folklore with emotional and sometimes comic reality. I was completely captivated by the rich, imaginative worlds created and felt the sheer magic as Finn and Ally make their heartfelt discoveries.

I remember telling everyone to make sure they see it!

Photo: Camilla Adams

1996

STEPPING STONES
by Mike Kenny

Winner of the Writers Guild Best Children's Play 1997.
Winner of Arts Council Children's Award in 2000.

Synopsis: This story goes from high noon hilltop heat haze to a snow-bound moonlit beach. Cynth, a young woman on a journey of change, is determined to find the fallen star for her Mam. Mam doesn't want Cynth to go, but Mam decides that she will help Cynth and secretly follows her on her journey. Both Cynth and her Mam encounter interesting characters on their journey, and find the home stone, the stepping stone, and the star stone. In the end, they learn that everything must grow and change.

Originally written for an audience of young people with learning disabilities, and performed by an integrated cast of actors with physical disabilities and sensory impairments.

"The stars in the sky
They seem to have always been
Suddenly one moves
And everything must change".

Originally produced by: Interplay, Leeds
Cast: 2F, 2M
Playing time: 1 hour 15 minutes
Audience recommendation: Young people with learning disabilities

Script available from: www.alanbrodie.com

Charles Way writes: It's a wonder to me that such a small play as this can be so huge. It's a magician's trick he's pulled off, and what begins as a charming story about leaving home and growing up becomes a tough nut of a play about real change – about the structures of life being remade through human love and need – from the scars and ashes of war.

Sometimes plays like this that are symbolic and universal lose their grip on an audience but not here. Each moment is recognisable on so many levels for children, adults and audiences with learning difficulties. It is written elegantly and sparely so that a director has plenty of time and space to create a sensory world that is as beautiful and as harsh as the lives depicted in the play, and yet it is without doubt fine dramatic literature. It is a quest play that is also domestic and it moves from nicely judged relational humour bordering on farce towards a bold dramatic revelation concerning the lives of its main protagonists Cynth and Mam.

Stepping Stones is a play which has not dated and sadly as groups of refugees struggle across Europe trying to rebuild their lives, it is as relevant as ever. A wonderful play that gives us the atavistic pleasure of a fireside story, told by a very modern playwright whose love of form and structure shines through his work.

1998

PLAYING FROM THE HEART
by Charles Way

Nominated by TMA for Best Children's Play.

Synopsis: Play with music, principally percussion.

A play about the childhood of world famous percussionist Evelyn Glennie.

A gritty, yet poetic, piece, which tells how Evelyn became a musician, despite becoming profoundly deaf between 8- and 12-years-old. The realistic narrative is linked by a series of imagistic set pieces, which explore the inner world of the deaf child.

The play explores themes of family love, overcoming impossible barriers and the very nature of art/music. It provides an opportunity to present a rich mix of movement, music and text.

Originally produced by: Polka Theatre

Cast: 3M, 2F and one percussionist.

Playing time: 1 hour 15 minutes

Audience recommendation: 8 years+

Script available from: info@aurorametro.com

Published in *Plays for Young People* (with *Eye of the Storm* and *Red Red Shoes*) Aurora Metro ISBN 0953675718

Nominated by: Vicky Ireland, Roman Stefanski

Vicky Ireland writes: When Artistic Director of Polka Theatre, I was always on the look out for stories of inspirational individuals to share with a young audience, and after listening to Evelyn Glennie on BBC Radio's Desert Island Discs, I immediately wrote to her to ask permission to create a play about her extraordinary early life. She in return, gave me her autobiography, *Good Vibrations* as a springboard.

I then turned to the wonderful writer Charles Way, and the resulting play he wrote, *Playing from the Heart*, is a beautiful tone poem-drama which explores Evelyn's early years, the illness that destroyed her hearing, and despite this, her astonishing achievement at becoming the first profoundly deaf artist to study percussion at the Royal School of Music. It details with wit and sensitivity how she discovered when her hearing had failed, that she could sense music through her skin and bones, and thus came to always play with her feet bare, to feel the vibrations of the sound she was making through contact with the floor.

An extraordinary person of huge talent and courage is captured in this fine play. There was a cherry on the cake for me. The actress who played Evelyn in my production migrated to New Zealand. After some time, she sent an email to say she had named her new baby daughter – Evelyn.

Photo: Polka Theatre

1998

THE BOY WHO FELL INTO A BOOK
by Alan Ayckbourn

Subsequently produced by the Soho Theatre, London as part of the Cultural Olympiad 2012.

Synopsis: Young Kevin is trapped in the pages of his favourite books, pursued by the villainous Green Shark with only his wits and his literary hero Rockfist Slim to help him escape.

Originally produced by: Stephen Joseph Theatre, Scarborough

Cast: 3F, 3M

Playing time: 1 hour 35 minutes, plus interval

Audience recommendation: 6 years+

Script available from: Faber (play)

Amateur: Details at www.samuelfrench-london.co.uk

Professional: Contact mel@casarotto.co.uk

Nominated by: Steve Marmion

Steve Marmion writes: Alan's work for and with young people has always had the same heart, rigour, humour and inventiveness as his more famous grown up work. This play has that style and innovation falling off it.

The Dragnet detective style grabs the adventurer in every child by the raincoat lapels and throws him into the greatest hits of children's fiction. Through the literary sampling and focusing of these classics, the immediate relevance to the life of the audience floods through, and the urge to grab a book is piqued. As is the urge to imagine, and play, and adventure.

An *Alice in Wonderland* for boys and book clubs.

(See Steve Marmion's article on Alan Ayckbourn's writing for young audiences.)

1999

UNDER THE APPLE TREE

by Dave Tarkenter, Paul Harman and Philip Harrison

Winner of Barclays TMA Award 2000 for Best Children's Play.

Synopsis: A theatrical adventure exploring all the senses, including smell and taste, celebrating the sound of words and the richness of colours.

Originally produced by: CTC (Cleveland Theatre Company), Darlington

Cast: 2 mature male actors.

Playing time: 45 minutes

Audience recommendation: 3–5 years

Script available from: paul.harman63@ntlworld.com

Available in German: www.theaterverlaghofmann-paul.de/ theaterstuecke/unter-dem-apfelbaum

Nominated by: Paul Harman

Paul Harman writes: Our aim was to present two male actors in nursery schools where females predominate and to offer an alternative view of men as playful and gentle. It was devised in the rehearsal room with text written to support the actions.

Wendy Meadley's design and making were both essential to meeting our objective to create a theatre event based not on narrative but on a sequence of sensations, visual and aural. For that we needed rich objects, like the seven foot high galvanised metal tree, on which we could hang individually crafted leaves and a large silver apple which opened out to show its seeds. There was a richly embroidered fish and a phoenix. There were candles over which a little pan with spices could be heated to fill the room with strange scents. The children sat on a large, silky quilt.

At the end, of course, everyone ate a piece of apple.

2000

SOULS
by Roy Williams

Synopsis: A funny, moving family drama about sibling relationships in a West Indian family. With their mother Pamela dead, brothers Derek, Stephen and Anthony are reunited with each other at the family home for her funeral.

Derek has been a car mechanic since he was 16 years old. He has his own garage. Anthony is a student, working part time in a burger bar. Stephen is a wheeler dealer, and spends most of his time evading the police. When Derek is in danger of losing his business, he allows himself to be persuaded by Stephen to go along with an elaborate insurance scam that will get him back in the money. Anthony is at first reluctant to get involved, but changes his mind when Stephen calls his baby brother a 'softie' and 'little mummy's boy'. What starts as a well laid plan becomes a long, dark journey for each of them as they try to come to terms their feelings of grief, pride, rage, loneliness and hope.

Roy Williams writes: For me, the play has always been about the character who isn't there – but her presence is felt throughout the entire piece – the Mother. She speaks for the Windrush generation who came to the UK in the late 40s, with such promise, only to encounter hatred and racism. In a few years, the Windrush generation will no longer exist, and tough things will be asked of the generation to follow. This is what I aimed to capture with *Souls*. That generation, represented by the three brothers in the piece, fighting within itself, to establish its own identity.

Originally produced by: Theatre Centre
Cast: 3M
Playing time: 1 hour
Audience recommendation: 12 years+
Script available from: info@aurorametro.com
Published in *Theatre Centre: Plays for Young People*
Nominated by: Paul Harman

2000

WALKING THE TIGHTROPE
by Mike Kenny

Winner of the 2009 Dora Mavor Award.

Synopsis: "Every year right at the end of summer just before the leaves turn brown and fall from the trees, Esme comes to stay with her Nanna and Granddad…" But this year something is different; Nanna Queenie is gone. Though Grandad and Esme do the fun activities they usually do, things aren't the same without Nanna Queenie. Grandad can't bring himself to say that Nanna has died, so he explains that Nanna has joined the circus. "She looked like an ordinary woman, but inside beat the heart of a tightrope walker."

Originally produced by: New Perspectives, UK

Cast: 1F, 1M

Playing time: 1 hour 15 minutes

Audience recommendation: all ages

Script available from: www.alanbrodic.com

Nominated by: Jonathan Lloyd, Miranda Thain, David Wood

Miranda Thain writes: Mike Kenny is undoubtedly one of the most significant contributors to the canon of plays for young audiences and, for me, *Walking the Tightrope* is one of his best – the perfect example of a small play with big ideas and a big heart.

Mike's words are few but beautifully chosen, the relationship between Esme and Granddad is expertly crafted and real, and the play's simplicity is underscored by a deep tenderness that is inclusive of the whole audience, grown-ups and children alike. A little gem of a play.

2001

TALKING WITH ANGELS
by Neil Duffield

Synopsis: The story of an extraordinary young woman, Joan of Arc, the real Joan, a teenager who first heard voices in the fields. In the space of less than a year, she propelled herself from unknown shepherd girl to French national heroine, scourge of the English and famed throughout Europe.

Originally produced by: Quicksilver Theatre Company, London

Cast: Minimum 2F, 2M, or up to 15

Playing time: 1 hour 10 minutes

Audience recommendation: 7 years+

Script available from: info@aurorametro.com in *Plays for Youth Theatres and Large Casts* by Neil Duffield (Aurora Metro)

Performing rights: n.duffield1@ntlworld.com

Nominated by: Carey English

Carey English writes: I am delighted that *Talking with Angels* by Neil Duffield has been included in this collection of plays, celebrating the fifty years of TYA playwriting in England.

Joan of Arc is a perennial symbol of freedom and heroism. The play follows her turbulent story and emotional journey through epoch-changing events and her impact on them. Specially written for children over 7 years old, *Talking with Angels* is set in contemporary times. With its themes of justice, empowerment and growing up, the play explores how, with true belief in yourself, the most ordinary person – a girl like you or a boy like me – can alter the course of history.

Great storytelling told in a humorous and thought-provoking way, the play is genuinely suited to all ages over 7. It got terrific feedback from school and family audiences including the priceless comment – "If all theatre was this good we would go every week."

2001

BREATHING SPACE
by Mary Cooper

Toronto Theatre Festival with British Council Sponsorship 2003. Shortlisted for a DORA Award for Best Touring Production 2003.

Synopsis: The story of a tentative romance between two 15-year-olds, brought together by exile and chance as next door neighbours in a small Northern town. Zara and her Mum, Marina, have fled war in Kosovo to seek asylum in Britain. Danny and his Mum, Linda, have run hundreds of miles to get away from Danny's violent dad. He'll kill Linda this time – if he finds her; Danny knows that. Last time she nearly died when his father put her in hospital with broken ribs and a punctured lung.

A poky flat with a stinking stairwell and bars on the windows is the last place Zara wants to be. She's left behind a plush house in Pristina, good friends, an elite school and her beloved father, to live in squalor among people who treat her like a half-wit.

Danny's got nothing. Zara's had everything laid on. At least that's what Danny hears from the lads who he meets at the bus stop on the first day at his new school. But when Danny breaks into Zara's flat encouraged by his new friends, he finds out more than he bargained for about her. Gradually, the two young people begin to realise they have more in common than they could ever have expected. And when the violent father finally tracks down Danny and Linda, it is to Zara and her mother that they must turn for refuge.

Originally produced by: M6 Theatre Company, Rochdale.
Cast: 3F, 1M
Playing time: 1 hour
Audience recommendation: 12 years+
Script available from: www.mary-cooper.co.uk/

Nominated by: Dot Wood

Dot Wood writes: Mary Cooper's gripping and deeply moving play, *Breathing Space* tells the story of two families experiencing the aftermath of violence and separation – one seeking sanctuary from domestic violence, the other from war.

I saw the play in many North West secondary schools and at a theatre festival in Toronto during 2002/2003. Commissioned by M6 Theatre Company, *Breathing Space* was written for teenage audiences.

The play tells of Danny and his mum, who are in hiding in a rundown flat in a strange town, scared to answer the phone or open the door for fear of Danny's abusive dad tracking them down. Kosovan asylum-seekers Zara and Marina, who move in next door, are anxiously awaiting news of the safety of Zara's father. On the surface the two families seem very different.

As the story unfolds we are drawn into their lives and begin to understand how much they have in common.

In workshops following the play, it was wonderful to hear young people sharing a deep understanding and empathy for the characters but also their passionate discussions about the different script and staging conventions that had economically and creatively communicated so much.

2001

RED RED SHOES

by Charles Way

Arts Council of England's Children's Award 2004.

Synopsis: The play is an adaptation of Hans Christian Andersen's dark tale of a young girl's desire to dance. It tells the story of Franvera who lives in a country 'so very near so very far away' who on her birthday is given a pair of red dancing shoes. When her country collapses into war and ethnic cleansing, the shoes become both her link with her old life and also a symbol of the trauma she suffers.

Originally produced by: The Unicorn Theatre and The Place

Cast: The play was originally written for a cast size of seven, but has also been performed by four, very energetic actor/dancers and by The City of London School for Girls with a cast of 40.

Playing time: 1 hour 15 minutes

Audience recommendation: 8–13 years

Script available from: info@aurorametro.com in *Plays for Young People* (with *Eye of the Storm* and *Playing from the Heart*).

A German translation is available from Theaterstückverlag München

Nominated by: Tony Graham, Nettie Scriven

Nettie Scriven writes: I selected *Red Red Shoes* for its beauty of storytelling and its haunting imagery. It is a particularly fine example of theatre at its best, of the fusion between dance and performance, and even better that is has been written for young people.

As a theatre designer working with theatre design students, I wanted them to tackle a play for young people, that is both sophisticated and dark in its content whilst having a poetic resonance that offered rich play for their imaginations.

The play is a designer's dream.

The language conjures potent images and embodies the rhythm and the movement in Franvera's feet in an epic retelling of a story about control, prohibition, hate and revenge which place a traumatised child, whose bones have turned to ice, at the centre of the world.

The play shows how theatre for young people can, and should, deal with powerful themes that reflect the world we live in, and the inner world of the child. The aftermath of war and the state of being a refugee are themes that are constantly present in the modern world, and Charlie's play, is still powerfully resonant today, fifteen years on from its original creation.

Photo: Chris Nash

2001

WARRIOR SQUARE
by Nick Wood

Brothers Grimm Prize, Berlin.

Synopsis: Riva and Andrea are at their new school in England. We jump back to their old school, in their home country. The teacher tells Andrea he must find his sister Riva, and leave school at once, without anyone seeing. As they rush away, they see two big black cars pulling into the school gates. 'And that's how it happens ... in the middle of an ordinary day ... the sky falls in.'

The family decide to leave. After three years on the run they arrive in Britain, but things are difficult. They cannot speak English, and have to live in a crumbling hotel in a seaside town, crammed together with hundreds of others – people from their own community, and from the one they were at war with in their home country. Riva tries her best to make friends, but Andrea is angry and confrontational. He loves to play football, but will only play by himself. Even when the other boys invite him to join their game, he fights them off. Finally the family are given permission to stay in England and we see them beginning, in small ways, to come to terms with what has happened to them.

Originally produced by: Nottingham Playhouse Roundabout Company

Cast: 1F, 1M (3-handed version also for Action Transport Theatre)

Playing time: 40 minutes approx.

Audience recommendation: 10 years+

Script available from: woodn55@gmail.com (Original version) info@aurorametro.com (3-handed version)

Published by: Aurora Metro Books www.aurorametro.com
European rights: engelmann@felix-bloch-erben.de
Nominated by: Andrew Breakwell

Andrew Breakwell writes: As I write, Sweden (!) is considering deporting, in chartered aircraft, almost half of the asylum seekers/refugees who have landed on their shores in the last year. Who would have thought fifteen years ago that the themes of *Warrior Square*, refuge, asylum, integration and diversity would still be appropriate for performances to children and young people? Arguably, they are even more relevant at a time when the UK Prime Minister announces that Britain will take in another 30,000 children from war-torn areas of the world.

Yet *Warrior Square* nearly didn't happen. I met Nick Wood when I arrived in Nottingham to be the Director of Roundabout TIE at Nottingham Playhouse. Nick was, at that time, still teaching in a secondary school and writing in his spare time. He was also the facilitator of a writing group at the Playhouse. After we'd met I asked him to send me an example of his work, which he dutifully did. The play showed craft in construction, a way with dialogue and characters which were interesting, but the subject matter didn't appeal.

I wrote to Nick saying thanks but no thanks, but maybe he'd like to come in and we could talk about a commission? He read 'thanks but no thanks' and despatched the letter to the bin. It was only some time later that he half-remembered that there was a line at the bottom he hadn't read. On such foundations are creative relationships built!

Warrior Square has secured itself a place in the repertoire of Theatre for Young People throughout continental Europe, but its first outing was also just by chance. Roundabout was invited to take *Stepping on the Cracks* by Mike Kenny to ASSITEJ in Germany. At the time, *Warrior Square* was also playing with the same actors. I suggested that both plays might be of interest. The standing ovation, for oh so many minutes after the performance in Frankfurt, was truly astonishing – neither the actors, Nick, nor I, quite knew what to do or what we had done!

Since then there have been numerous productions and manifestations of the text, some that are indeed a surprise to the author – structure, dialogue and characters being somewhat fluid. However, the unifying element is that the play speaks to everyone, from whatever nation or culture, about this important issue. Even recently, warring factions and nations claim the story as their own.

Here in the UK, it gives our young audiences a unique insight into what might have happened to the new arrivals who have joined their school and who have the strange language, the hand-me-down clothes and that far-away look in their eyes. Yet sadly, because of changes in education policies, few in this country will have the opportunity to see a production, as neither the curriculum nor timetable permits. So it is in this volume that the phenomenon that is *Warrior Square* is celebrated.

Author's note: 23 further productions have been made since winning the Brüder Grimm Prize for its first German production (Fluchtwege) at Hans Otto Theater, Potsdam. It's been seen in Moscow and Korea, and the Croatian and Sarajevo (Trg Ratnika) productions toured extensively in Eastern Europe.

Photo: Gerry Murray

2001

HANNAH AND HANNA

by John Retallack

Edinburgh Festival Winner of Herald Angel Award TMA Award / Best New Show for Young People nominee 2004–2005.

Synopsis: Having escaped from Pristina, Hanna, meets Hannah, from Margate. An unlikely friendship develops when they find that music is a common bond between them despite their different cultures and circumstances.

Originally produced by: Company of Angels and Channel Theatre Company, Margate.

Cast: Hannah, 16, from UK and Hanna, 16, from Kosovo. They play all the supporting roles.

Playing time: 40 minutes first half, 40 minutes second half, total 80 minutes.

Audience recommendation: 13+

Script available from: Samuel French Ltd.

It is also published in different editions by Oberon, by English Centre and by Samuel French Ltd., and in French by Editions Fontaine.

Translated and produced in French, Swedish, German, Dutch, Portuguese, Hebrew and Japanese

Nominated by: Vicky Ireland

Teresa Ariosto writes: I saw *Hannah and Hanna* for the first time at Battersea Arts Centre in February 2002 where it was part of the *Time Out* Critics' Choice Season. I had just started to work for Company of Angels and wasn't sure what to expect…

It was a great experience, the audience was spellbound throughout the show and the moment in which Hannah and Hanna become friends is still, for me, a highlight, constantly reminding me of the magic of theatre.

After that January, Company of Angels' production of *Hannah and Hanna* toured venues and schools across the UK for three consecutive years and it was brought to India, the Philippines and Malaysia by the British Council. The play was translated and produced in Belgium, France, Sweden, Germany, Holland and Israel.

Since then I have seen the play dozens of time, with different casts, in different languages, with different audiences, and I've always invariably felt that its mixture of intense sentiment and tough reality goes straight to your heart allowing that special connection with the characters which few plays manage to achieve.

Although *Hannah and Hanna* is set in a particular time and place and clearly deals with the Kosovar tragedy at the end of the 90s, it couldn't be more topical at a time where an unprecedented refugee crisis is shaking Europe and the entire world. The play reminds us that we are human beings above all and that cultural differences can be overcome and similarities embraced. It is more important than ever for young people to see it.

2001

MY LONG JOURNEY HOME

Devised by NIE Company

Nominated for Best Ensemble Performance, Edinburgh Fringe 2004.

Synopsis: *My Long Journey Home* is based on the true story of Andras Tomas, a Hungarian boy who was press-ganged into the Wehrmacht in 1942, taken to fight on the Eastern Front and then lost in Russia for fifty-three years. Andras finally returned home to a hero's welcome in 1999. Using live accordion and violin, clowning and comedy, singing and tragedy, one small puppet and a simple set, *My Long Journey Home* conjures up a vast and impossible world and a cacophony of languages.

Originally produced by: NIE
Cast: 4M
Playing time: 1 hour
Audience recommendation: All
Script available from: www.nie-theatre.com/
Nominated by: Kate Cross

Alex Byrne writes: New International Encounter (NIE) has always devised as a group working together. The writing down of the show followed after the show had opened, sometimes many months after. The play was written in the room, on the floor, on our feet. In the end I decided what was in and out, how the story would be structured as a play, how to begin and end, but the play is owned by all of the people who made it. Of course it also changed along the way – we played over 400 performances and each was different. We were striving for a theatre that was alive, in the moment and with and for its audience on that day in that place. The show has had over 460 reprises in 15 countries and is now only played as part of the *European Narratives Trilogy*, together with *Past Half Remembered* and *The End of Everything Ever*.

Kate Cross, director of the egg, Theatre Royal Bath, writes: *The End of Everything Ever* was the first play by NIE that I had seen. My hunch is that the company did not set out to make a show for a young audience, rather that they wanted to create a theatrical work about a true, historical event. People who saw it would then place it, time and again, in front of a young audience.

By the time I saw this play, it was a well-crafted one. The protagonist's journey was relayed in a series of unfortunate happenings, each lending peril, poignancy and tragedy to the storytelling: perfect ingredients for a thrilling and gripping theatrical ride.

Lyn Gardner wrote of it: "It begins with music that makes you want to dance and ends in a silence so loud you wish you could turn it down." – *The Guardian*

Yes! If you are going to make theatre about tragic events, then you should dare to be funny, dare to be zany and dare to be irreverent. That is what this multi-cultural group have done, between them co-owning their horrendous historical legacy. Out of the chaos and anarchy of their now familiar style, the sadness, the loneliness and the hope become all the more, stark and chilling.

2001

JUMPING ON MY SHADOW
by Peter Rumney

Winner of the John Whiting Award for Best Play in 2002, the only play written specifically for young people to win this prestigious prize.

Synopsis: *Jumping on my Shadow* is a history play, ghost story, and tragicomedy, inspired by the many-layered immigrant histories of London's Brick Lane. We begin with the smell of baking bread. Three generations of refugees and migrants inhabit the same bakery, but at different periods in time. Their stories collide in the bakery, and across time. The children try to come to terms with growing up in the adult world. Adults are forced to question the lies and innocence that have sustained them over the year and all the while, bread, a metaphor for the cultural richness that immigrants have always brought to Britain, continues to rise and bake in the oven.

The audience are invited to empathise with the feelings of disenfranchisement that can lead to racist attitudes. But they are asked to understand that it is both moral and utilitarian to welcome immigrants into a society. This conflict of perspective is encapsulated in the final image of the play. We all have to stand up for what we believe in, but at what price?

Originally produced by: Theatre Centre
Cast: 2F, 2M
Playing time: 1 hour
Audience recommendation: 8 years+
Script available from: Faber & Faber
Nominated by: Nettie Scrivens

Rosamunde Hutt writes: In 1996 Theatre Centre moved right next door to London's Brick Lane. We found ourselves in a site steeped in history, walking in the footsteps of the Huguenot silk weavers, Jewish refugees, the protestors fighting the Blackshirts on Cable Street, and stopping for a delicious curry at Sweet and Spicy. I knew we needed a play to capture the vibe of this remarkable place. Peter Rumney's grandfather had worked on Brick Lane during the war and with his passion about the politics of immigration I knew that Peter was the man for the job. The play opens with the smell of baking bread as three sets of refugees inhabit a bakery at different points in time. This was inspired by the mosque in Brick Lane that had been a synagogue and before that a church. A boy from nowhere is catapulted into the city with nothing but the memory of the smell of his mother's cooking and his lively wit to sustain him. In 2000 headlines screamed, 'No Room at the Inn'. In 2016 all and nothing has changed. Across Europe we have seen heart-stopping generosity, doors opened, refugees embraced, but we have also seen fences built, hostility and despair. This is a play for our times.

Photo: Hugo Glendinning

2002

DIARY OF AN ACTION MAN
by Mike Kenny

Synopsis: Young Ezra has two memories of his father: he was a British Sign Language user and he was a soldier. Ezra uses his Action Man figurine to bring an alternative version of his dad to life. This dream is smashed by Mum trying to introduce her new boyfriend to Ezra and his sister Louise. This sends Ezra on a mission: to save Dad. With the help of his friend Spud, he gets to Manchester and finds his dad: an ordinary bloke who is the opposite of what an Action Man represents. But how do Mum and Dad reconcile their differences for the sake of their children?

Originally produced by: Graeae Theatre & Unicorn Theatre, London

Cast: 2F, 3M

Playing time: 1 hour 30 minutes

Audience recommendation: 7 years+

Script available from: www.alanbrodie.com

Nominated by: Amit Sharma

Amit Sharma writes: This is a wonderful play, which deals with family, war, adventure, disability, love, dreams, mental health and an Action Man!

Interweaving British Sign Language and live audio description as part of the text, and cleverly written like pages of a diary, it's a tender play that deals with big issues for young audiences in an immensely creative, dynamic and fun way.

2003

SHOPPING FOR SHOES
by Tim Crouch

Arts Council Brian Way Award 2007.

Synopsis: A romantic comedy, exploring the power of the logo and how hard it is to resist.

Siobhan McCluskey, a politically aware 13-year-old vegetarian, has a crush on fellow pupil, Shaun Holmes, who only cares about his Nike Air Jordans. They are brought together following a chance encounter with some dog dirt and a trip to a bowling alley.

Crouch performed the piece using a platform tilted towards the audience, on which he places pairs of shoes representing the characters. 'The shoes are never animated like conventional puppets, but each is given time, space and sometimes sound to assert itself.' So Siobhan's dad, Keith, is represented by 'Terrible sandals and jaunty whistling.'

Originally produced by: The Education Department of the Royal National Theatre.

Cast: 1M (originally performed by Tim Crouch)

Playing time: 45 minutes

Audience recommendation: 11 years+

Script available from: Faber & Faber.

For performance rights, contact Giles Smart gsmart@ unitedagents.co.uk

Nominated by: Vicky Ireland

Douglas Irvine, Artistic Director of Visible Fictions writes: The first time I read *Shopping for Shoes*, I fell in love with so many things about it: its accessibility, its storytelling, its humour, its vibrant politics – and I just knew our company had to create a version of it. It's a wonderful piece of writing and through that production, which many years later is still in demand, I've seen just how profoundly it connects to a young audience: reflecting their world and experience whilst giving them so much to think about.

The story tells of a romance that develops between two young people who at first sight wouldn't be obviously suited – one a political activist and one a shoe 'fashionista' – and it's so charmingly executed, cleverly plotted, and rich with ideas yet so clear and simple. And it has an ending of such transcendent beauty that the heart is left warmed and complete.

A theatre director friend summed up the play with these words: "It's a play where nothing of consequence seems to happen yet everything of consequence happens."

This statement captures just some of the essence, beauty and joy of *Shopping for Shoes*. I hope you enjoy it.

2004

THE GARDENER
by Mike Kenny

Synopsis: This is a story that is being forgotten and remembered at the same time. As the leaves fall from the branches of Harry's fading memory they turn into the green shoots of Joe's new stories.

Joe has a new baby sister and nobody wants to play with him. Nobody wants to play with old Uncle Harry either so together they begin to work on Uncle Harry's garden. Even if Uncle Harry can't remember ordinary things, he and Joe create a year to remember.

Originally produced by: AJTC and Nottingham Roundabout, UK

Cast: 2M

Playing time: 50 minutes

Audience recommendation: All ages

Script available from: www.alanbrodie.com

Mick Jasper of AJTC writes: Of all our productions *The Gardener* is the one that has elicited the most heartfelt reactions from young and old alike. It is an apparently simple tale of a grumpy old man (Harry) and his angry nephew (Joe), who eventually find a way to tolerate one another. As with all of Mike's work there is much more to it than that.

Beneath the silliness that breaks out at every opportunity, beneath the rhymes and rhythms and repetitions, beneath the eventual triumphant transformation of the garden is a grounding of deep emotional truth. It is a story that is being forgotten and remembered at the same time. As the leaves fall from the branches of Harry's fading memory they turn into the green shoots of Joe's new stories.

This is a play for children that adults also relate to.

2006

BLUE
by Tim Webb

Synopsis: *Blue* is inspired by the sounds and images of blues music. It is not one of Oily Cart Theatre's most radical pieces, but it gives a real taste of its ability to communicate directly with its audience – young people with severe disabilities and their carers.

A tented space with its swing seats and rocking chairs has the feel of a station porch somewhere in the Deep South. Here as we wait for the train, musicians sing and play while the passengers reveal the contents of their luggage: water to splash, stars to handle, a fan to create a cool breeze, a video camera to capture the image of a laughing child being serenaded. What's interesting about the work is the way it breaks down all the traditional barriers between performer and audience and the rules that cast the actors as active and the audience as passive. The show opens with children offering up the contents of their own 'blue boxes' of precious memories and objects.

This is not a theatrical experience you watch, but one that you share.

Originally produced by: Oily Cart in London Special Schools and other public venues

Cast: The original cast contained only one woman (Belle) and five men. There could just as easily have been five women and one man but they would all have to be good singers. All the characters could have come out of the lyrics of blues songs.

Playing time: 50 minutes

Audience recommendation: 3–19 but all for young people who were either classified as having Profound and Multiple Learning Disabilities (PMLD) or as having an Autistic Spectrum Condition (ASC)

Script available from: oilies@oilycart.org.uk

The text is available in Oily Cart: *All Sorts of Theatre for All Sorts of Kids*, M. Brown (ed), (Trentham Books), London 2012.

Nominated by: Jonathan Lloyd

Jonathan Lloyd writes: Walking into the auditorium for a performance of *Blue* I was transported into a uniquely warm and welcoming world.

Like so much of Oily Cart's work, this spell was cast with the deftest of means: beautiful blues music, some simple props, striking and evocative costumes, hammocks for members of the audience to swing in and stories told clearly, intimately, directly, as if conjured just for you, on that morning, as if for the first time. It was an experience that's lingered long in my memory.

2006

THE MONSTER UNDER THE BED
by Kevin Dyer

Synopsis: A boy meets the Monster who lives under his bed. Ben is having a difficult time – he's fallen out with his best mate at school, Vince – and his dad is away (he's a soldier in the army).The Monster says he'll go to school in Ben's place and sort out all his troubles – especially Vince. He puts on Ben's uniform and goes off with Ben's Mum.

We soon realise the Monster knows nothing of the outside world – and there will be much trouble ahead. Also, whilst the Monster is at school, the Monster's Dad, who also lives under the bed, is not happy – and drags Ben under the bed. The Monster's dad says he will hold Ben hostage until his son comes back. This seems OK – until the boy Monster loses his way home from school. So Ben has to persuade Monster Dad to leave the safety of the under-bed world and go into the city to bring back his son. That's quite an adventure for a monster that has never been outside.

An adventure story about facing your fears.

Originally produced by: Polka Theatre
Cast: 1F, 4M
Playing time: 1 hour 20 minutes
Audience recommendation: 6 years+
Script available from: info@aurorametro.com
Aurora Metro ISBN 9781906582074
Nominated by: Stephen Midlane, Jonathan Lloyd

Jonathan Lloyd writes: I'm a great believer that new plays for young audiences can and should be bold, resonant but also exciting, playful and wildly imaginative. I remember reading an early draft after I'd started my job as Artistic Director of Polka Theatre, a theatre with a proud tradition of staging brilliant new work for children.

Here was a play that set my pulse racing: an urgent story about a boy called Ben whose father was away at war but also a funny, scary tale about a monster living under Ben's bed, with his own dad trouble.

Kevin Dyer's a writer who cares passionately about telling ambitious, important stories that refuse to patronise his audience; and telling them in a way that's as exciting, entertaining and enjoyable as possible.

Photo: Hannah Milner

COSMOS

by Peter Rumney

Nottingham and Nottinghamshire Creative Business Awards 2009.

Shortlisted Brian Way Award for Young People's Playwriting 2010.

Synopsis: *Cosmos* is an immersive experience and participatory performance. A fusion of poetry, contemporary and Bharatanatyam dance, digital projection, music, and epic visual narrative. *Cosmos* explores complex and profound cosmological concepts with very young children.

The audience follow a child through the cosmos, towards the outer reaches of the solar system, on a quest to find her lost Story Star (her mother). They climb to the moon, explore the infinite enormity of space through grains of sand, and discover weightlessness as they are swept off their feet and danced in orbit round the sun.

The text is in two languages, English and Konnakol, the percussive notation language of South Asian music and dance. Konnakol was used both to create a familiar soundscape, and to explore the communication of emotion through pure spoken sound.

Originally produced by: Dragon Breath Theatre / Curve, Leicester / Nottingham Trent University

Cast: 5 performers (actors/dancers)

Playing time: 50 minutes

Audience recommendation: 4–6 years

Script available from: www.dragonbreaththeatre.com

Nominated by: Adel al Salloum

Adel al Salloum writes: The wonderful thing about *Cosmos* is that it is big in its endeavour. Dragon Breath Theatre creates visually stunning poetry – textually rich in many forms. The visual is as critical to Peter Rumney as the words and poetry.

When you work alongside Peter and Nettie Scriven (co-director and scenographer) you are at liberty to play around with multiple forms of poetry – the colour of an idea, the weight of a word or prop, the hand-held image of stardust projected onto sand.

Peter wonderfully knits together complex ideas about the wonders of the universe through ancient forms of Bharatnatyam and Konnakol rhythms. He creates space and time to explore the visual poetry as well as the real dancing rhymes and rhythms of the story.

And at the centre of these ideas and forms, that are strung together quite beautifully, you follow a simple story of a girl. A girl on a journey to a star. *Cosmos* was a theatrical event, an all-encompassing world of sound, image and light and a rare opportunity to feel like you really have travelled to a star.

Photo: Kerry James

2011

CINDERELLA

by Sally Cookson, Adam Peck and the Company

Best production for young people (Off West End Awards) 2014.

Synopsis: When Ella's mother dies, she is brought up by her father who teaches her all about the woodland birds that surround their home. All is well until her father remarries, when Ella has to live with a stern and manipulative Stepmother, a vain and bossy Stepsister, and a Stepbrother who copies his older sister in everything. After Ella's father dies, her life becomes even grimmer and the birds in the wood seem her only friends. Escaping to the woods one day, Ella meets a stranger who is bird watching. When he leaves, he gives her an invitation…

Ella is helped by the birds and her wicked stepmother is violently repaid for her cruelty.

The familiar story is given many original twists and includes events and atmosphere found in the earliest versions of the story in European literature.

Originally produced by: Tobacco Factory Theatres and Travelling Light Subsequently produced at St James Theatre and Unicorn Theatre, London

Cast: 2F, 3M and 2 musicians

Playing time: 2 hours including interval

Audience recommendation: 6 years+

Script available from: Adam Peck adzpeck@hotmail.com Oberon Books

Nominated by: Jude Merrill

Jude Merrill writes: This was one of those shows created through devising with a company of talented artists in which, magically, no-one falls out and everything comes together in perfect harmony.

Director Sally Cookson, having lost her own mother some months previously, wanted to make a show in which the spirit of the dead mother comforts and guides her daughter through the trials of a bleak life. In the end, the process pushed the doomed father into that role, and his tenderness for his motherless child is heartbreaking.

After his death, the birds that he taught her to love become Ella's friends, allies and guides, replacing the better-known Fairy Godmother from the Perrault version of the tale. Ella is taunted, not by the familiar Ugly Sisters, but by a stepsister bullied into viciousness by her mother, and a stepbrother so cowed by his place at the bottom of the pecking order that he is grateful for the first sign of humanity, and becomes Ella's scared and secret protector.

Undaunted by her un-loving step family, Ella is able to escape to her forest friends where she meets, and helps, an incompetent bird spotter. This of course is the Prince incognito, and the way in which the birds outwit the stepmother and get the two together at the ball is the stuff of legend. The stepmother's efforts to win the Prince for one of her children – or even herself – leave the audience in hysterics.

Through a mixture of familiar themes and inspired invention, the play leads its audiences on an emotional dance of laughter and tears, leaving us guessing right to the end whether our heroine will reappear in time to reclaim her rhinestone-studded boot.

2013

TREE CHILD
by Joseph Coelho

Synopsis: Every library has a deep dark corner where a child can become lost in another world. A corner, where trees can become monsters, where squirrels can become wicked and where tales of family can become rooted.

Tree Child is a story of growing up, of learning to live with life's knots and gnarls and seeking out its blossoms. This mythical adventure follows the journey of Delilah as she confronts the recent passing of her father in a strange, magical world hidden in a library.

Originally produced by: The Spark Arts for Children, Leicester

Cast: 1 Librarian/Narrator, Delilah (11–12 years old), Squirrel, The Tree Monster

Playing time: 50 minutes

Audience recommendation: 8 years+

Script available from: felicitytrew@carolinesheldon.co.uk

Nominated by: Adel al-Salloum

Adel al-Salloum writes: This play was such a joy to see realised. It was commissioned to be presented in libraries so we knew from the outset there would be limitations around production aesthetics. But this never once stopped Joseph imagining the unimaginable – the mythical world between the bookshelves.

Tree Child is subtle, simple and very domestic to begin with and the story and characters invite us in to an everyday reality. It's not long though until we follow a path (imagined) into a world between worlds to find characters and creatures that belong in a mythical place far beyond that of the carpeted library.

What is wonderful about *Tree Child* is that it is a metaphor for the library. Joseph didn't just create a story set in a library he created the experience that happens when you open a book too. A wonderful piece of storytelling, bold and vivid and full of escapism.

Without fail a child would ask of our storyteller at the end of a show 'so are you the librarian or not' and who were we to say?

Photo: Pamela Raith Photography

2013

WHOLE

by Philip Osment

Synopsis: Dylan, Chantal, Holly and Joseph went to school together but confusion about sexual identity and religion caused their relationships to fracture leading to Holly's eventual disappearance from their lives.

Four years later, Dylan, Chantal and Joseph have contacted a producing theatre company in order to present a play about those events and Nathalie has been employed to portray Holly. In the course of the play, we come to understand what happened to Holly, but when Dylan stops the play to make new revelations it results in an argument that jeopardises the performance and threatens to destroy their friendships.

Audiences are led to believe that this argument is 'for real' and that the actors are in real life the characters whom they are playing.

Originally produced by: 20 Stories High at the Unity Theatre, Liverpool

Cast: 2F, 2M

Playing time: 1 hour 25 minutes

Audience recommendation: 8 years+

Script available from: www.alanbrodie.com

Published by Oberon Books info@oberonbooks.com

Nominated by: Joe Coelho

Joe Coelho writes: A play that subtly and convincingly draws out the relationships of four friends in their teens. We believe in their escapades in the graveyard and can relate to the very familiar teen interactions that determine the young adults the characters will become.

This is a beautifully real play, not only in its ability to invite us into the world of these teens but also in its ability to totally destroy the fourth wall as we are led into the throes of a very real and immediate argument.

During the play you feel like you are seeing these young people grow before your eyes and so as the tragedy unfolds and we learn more of what becomes of Holly we can't help but feel like we have let down a friend. This is a wholly necessary, immediate and timely play that needs to be seen for young and old alike. It is also a piece that has a wonderful grasp of language as we see the teens jam and sing and recite poetry that is both totally of their age and yet also manages to transcend their age.

2014

MUCKY PUP
by Daniel Jamieson

Synopsis: Ben is a bright but anxious only-child who has trouble making friends and hates dirt. One weekend his mum has the bright idea of borrowing a dog – Chatty. Ben is distraught and insists his mum takes Chatty back next day, but in the night Ben discovers Chatty can talk.

An extremely mucky day unfolds in which boy and dog become unlikely friends, but also Chatty unwittingly helps Ben make friends with some other boys his own age. But when they get home, Ben is devastated to discover he can't keep Chatty.

In the end though, Ben has a wonderful surprise – several months later he's allowed to have one of Chatty's puppies and when no-one else is listening, Ben discovers it can talk too! He calls him Gabble and they become inseparable, because although Ben still hates dirt and Gabble rolls on the occasional dead squirrel, they both accept each other exactly the way they are.

Originally produced by: Theatre Alibi

Cast: 1F, 2M

Playing time: 50 minutes

Audience recommendation: 5–10 years +

Script available from: www.theatrealibi.co.uk

Nominated by: Kate Cross

Annemarie Macdonald writes: *Mucky Pup* touches on a subject that is familiar to many children, parents and teachers alike. When a young boy who wants life to be ordered and clean is thrown together with a fantastically grubby and anarchic dog, an unlikely friendship develops. Daniel's play, which is gloriously funny, as well as very moving, looks at the real importance of experiencing life to the full.

As with all of his work, Dan's characters are wonderfully engaging and sympathetic. The piece revels in the chaos that ensues when the unlikely pair spend time together, and Dan's experience shines through as he carefully deals with the difficulties faced by a child who feels a desperate need for order.

Photo: Steve Tanner

2015

HIDDEN

by Kevin Dyer

Synopsis: James is 13. He lives at home with his mum and his sister Katy. His mum is unwell and spends most days in bed and rarely leaves the house. James makes sure Katy has eaten her breakfast, brushes her hair, helps her with her homework, then takes her to school.

At the end of the day, he takes her home, cooks, tidies, sees mum. He runs between one and the other, playing table-tennis, talking to his mum, feeding his fish and burning the custard.

He is everything to everyone. Always.

Inspired by the stories of young carers, the play gives an insight into the issues around being a young person who cares and how that impacts on growing up.

Originally produced by: Theatre Hullabaloo, Darlington, in association with Inspired Youth under the title *Tiny Treasures*.

Cast: 1F, 1M

Playing time: 1 hour

Audience Recommendation: 9–13 years

Nominated by: Paul Harman

Paul Harman writes: A perfect example of UK professional Theatre for Young Audiences, the genre that fifty years ago was TIE or YPT. It is simple in its structure and staging and essentially a piece of storytelling addressed directly to an audience – not a fourth wall. It demands of an adult actor the humility to represent a younger person with such respect that children will never ask why an adult is pretending to be one of them. The subject matter is of contemporary relevance to many young people and the theatre-makers are implicitly asking them to share responsibility for an issue which adults cannot 'solve'.

Photo : Kevin Curran, Theatre Hullabaloo and Inspired Youth

PLAYS FOR YOUNG CHILDREN

1976 THE GINGERBREAD MAN by David Wood
1979 TOWN MOUSE AND COUNTRY MOUSE
  by Vicky Ireland
1982 PEACEMAKER by David Holman
1995 HOW HIGH IS UP? by Brendan Murray
1995 A SPELL OF COLD WEATHER by Charles Way
1999 UNDER THE APPLE TREE
  by Dave Tarkenter, Paul Harman, Philip Harrison
2000 WALKING THE TIGHTROPE by Mike Kenny
2001 JUMPING ON MY SHADOW by Peter Rumney
2004 THE GARDENER by Mike Kenny
2005 BLUE by Tim Webb
2009 COSMOS by Peter Rumney
2013 TREE CHILD by Joseph Coelho
2013 WHOLE by Philip Osment

PLAYS FOR CHILDREN (8+)

1973 DRINK THE MERCURY by David Holman

1981 CHAIRPERSON by Geoff Bullen

1983 UNDER EXPOSURE by Lisa Evans

1984 NO WORRIES by David Holman

1985 GETTING THROUGH
by Nona Shepphard and Bryony Lavery

1987 WHISPERS IN THE DARK by Noël Grieg

1988 ROSIE BLITZ by Richard Pinner

1989 INVISIBLE FRIENDS by Alan Ayckbourn

1990 THE FLOOD by Charles Way

1994 HOOD IN THE WOOD by Noël Grieg

1995 INTO THE WEST by Greg Banks

1996 STEPPING STONES by Mike Kenny

1998 THE BOY WHO FELL INTO A BOOK
by Alan Ayckbourn

1998 PLAYING FROM THE HEART by Charles Way

2001 TALKING WITH ANGELS by Neil Duffield

2001 RED RED SHOES by Charles Way

2002 DIARY OF AN ACTION MAN by Mike Kenny

2006 THE MONSTER UNDER THE BED by Kevin Dyer

2011 CINDERELLA
by Sally Cookson, Adam Peck and the Company

2014 MUCKY PUP by Daniel Jamieson

2015 HIDDEN by Kevin Dyer

PLAYS FOR YOUNG PEOPLE (13+)

1977 NO PARASAN by David Holman

1978 OPERATION ELVIS by C.P. Taylor

1980 STRONGER THAN SUPERMAN by Roy Kift

1981 BLOOD BROTHERS by Willy Russell

1984 RAJ
by Leeds Playhouse Theatre in Education Company

1986 SHOUTING, STAMPING AND SINGING HOME
by Lisa Evans

1988 BAG DANCING by Mike Kenny

1992 DREAMS OF ANNE FRANK by Bernard Kops

1994 THE BOMB by Kevin Dyer

1994 BRETEVSKI STREET by Lin Coghlan

2000 SOULS by Roy Williams

2001 BREATHING SPACE by Mary Cooper

2001 WARRIOR SQUARE by Nick Wood

2001 HANNAH AND HANNA by John Retallack

2001 MY LONG JOURNEY HOME
devised by NIE Company

2003 SHOPPING FOR SHOES by Tim Crouch

THE WRITERS SPEAK

Alan Ayckbourn

"There is a joke, which I think I may have started, that I'm rewriting all my adult plays for kids. 'This is gentler. You don't send the little girl stark raving mad…' I'm also trying to retain as much as possible the colours that I put into the adult plays. That is, I would like them to try a little – not too much – I would like them to laugh, of course, and to be excited, and to be afraid, but not so they can't sleep. My ulterior motive is to excite the children into coming back when they're 25, so we haven't got another lost generation saying: 'the theatre is something I don't understand."

(Daily Telegraph, 17 November 1989)

"I wanted to write entertaining, intelligent plays that children would like, that would give them a full range of emotional experiences. It wouldn't be just a lot of custard being poured over each other (although I'm a huge Laurel and Hardy fan and I think custard is great!). I want plays to be a bit frightening, a bit sad, a bit everything – all things adult. I used to write about one play a year until I began with these children's plays, which are beginning to occupy me more and more. Now, very careful scheduling is allowing me to write two plays a year – a family play and an adult play. It's liberating to work in a different form, and this children's work is affecting my adult work, which is very interesting. Writing for kids makes you feel a bit more daring – you can depart from the curse of realism. I've started to float away a bit – as in *Body Language* and in *Wildest Dreams* – and I hope the adults will come with me."

(*The Hull Journal*, 1990)

"We were doing the odd children's show before that (*Mr A's Amazing Maze Plays*), but they always seemed a bit gungey to me. You threw your brain out of the window to do them. And I was watching some of the kids coming to the adult drama, sitting through pretty heavy stuff. I thought, what's the big deal with kid's drama? Perhaps the plays have to be fractionally shorter, and I think you don't want to leave the children emotionally scarred – but otherwise it's probably much nearer to adult drama than I thought it was. Which I suppose is a bit like discovering the wheel really, after writing for so long! ...

"I call it *Woman In Mind* for children. Then in *Callisto 5* the little boy has only a robot for company. That was my *Henceforward...* for children. The running joke is that I'm rewriting all my canon for children – but I don't think it's quite got to that stage...

"A lot of my plays are about people who attempt to find alternative existences outside their real lives. Because their real lives are so boring or so sad...

"Children's plays are about the basics. And a lot of my adult plays these days, when you boil them down a bit, are about the basics – about good and evil. In *Man of the Moment* you have evil meeting good. I've met people who are positive, good, life-asserting people who enliven and lift the people around them, and bad people, who do the reverse. It's often denied, but I do believe there is a spiritual tide that runs both ways. So I'm exploring that and going back to basics – in several senses...

"I think in a way, without false modesty, that writing for children requires truly phenomenal experience. You have to do everything you do for adults, only you have to do it slightly better. Adults will give you about five minutes. They say, 'Well, it's a bit slow, but it'll probably warm up.' Children will give you quarter of a second. Then they say 'Boring!' and turn round to talk to the person behind. It's a very good, refresher course in writing drama. You can get a bit sloppy writing for adults because you can get away with a lot. I think children's drama needs to be respectable-ised a bit, done by a few of our top dramatists."

(*The Independent*, 6 March 1991)

"You have to be responsible and try to say something positive, whereas in adult plays you can be a bit more despairing and finish up on a negative ... They [certain aspects of children's theatre] assume that the only things that will attract children are the very, very loud and the very, very crude, mostly in terms of wide slapstick. Children can take fear, they can take excitement, they can take tension, they can take sorrow. They can take Bambi's mother dying. One hopes that the spectrum of emotion isn't filtered out...

"I've been slowly moving towards a much more graphic narrative style and the plays have got much bigger in their field, much darker, and more fantastic. And for fantastic, read childlike."

(*Evening Standard*, 8 March 1991)

"*Invisible Friends* in the end is probably just as serious as *Woman In Mind*. I suppose, the moral I have, when writing a children's show, is don't shut the door on them in terms of options because it seems to me that if one has any faith in the human race, it is just conceivable that the next generation may solve the problems that we and our predecessors have singularly failed to solve."

(Interview, 1992)

"Lucy has a family but she is very lonely and she feels alienated. I had an invisible friend when I was young, quite a lot of people I know did at some point, and they were real and very annoying for parents. They had to lay an extra place at table and had to acknowledge that Tim – that was my friend – that Tim was sitting there. It's not a rare phenomenon. But it's also interesting that that particular play, *Invisible Friends*, as somebody pointed out, is a child's version of a play of mine called *Woman in Mind*, which is a much grimmer piece but nevertheless not a million miles away in theme. In both cases, they show the dangers of living your fantasy life at the expense of your real life and how you can get into some sort of trouble by confusing the two. In Lucy's time, it became a moral fable about trying to love the people you live with, rather than the people you invent. Like how the most awful brother can be all right in the end."

(Personal correspondence, 1999)

"We had a magic vase in *Invisible Friends* that appeared to move across the table on its own. It was incredible and very well done. Our master carpenter built this wonderful device. No one could see how it worked. Everybody after the show, because it was in the round, would crawl around trying to find out how it was done. To no avail. In the show, the vase would be sitting there on the table and suddenly it would move apparently of its own volition. Or rather when a character was told to concentrate on it and will it to move. At the end, the audience were asked to make the vase move. You could see the kids who were sort of going 'Nah, this is stupid' but concentrated despite themselves, sort of giving it the benefit of the doubt. When suddenly the thing moved, you could see them going; 'Oh, my God! Maybe I did make it move.'"

(Personal correspondence, 1999)

"I think I write from the adult's perspective. I don't try to become a child. I try and imagine what I as a child would have enjoyed and what my children would have enjoyed. I think initially I did write consciously for children but I hardly do that now, providing I feel the theme is right for them. I obviously make certain adjustments. I don't write things that I think would not interest them, like sexual politics – particularly for the young ones, you know, that's just baffling.

On the whole, I've discovered that children have the same needs from theatre as adults. You just have to be careful how you deal with them. They like to be frightened; they like to be excited, they don't just want to laugh, any more than adults just want to laugh. I think these days I write entirely from my own perspective but just bring out the child in me – it's difficult to explain. The worst thing I could do, which I'm very afraid of, would be to patronise children… lower myself to them. I think that it is better to write above them than below them, so that they have to reach a little. I think they will do that."

(Personal correspondence, 1999) © Copyright: Alan Ayckbourn

Steve Marmion writes: Alan's work for (and with) younger people has always had the same heart, rigour, humour and inventiveness as his more famous grown up work. *The Boy who Fell into a Book* (alongside *Mr A's Amazing Maze Plays*), has that style and innovation falling off it.

The Dragnet detective style grabs the adventurer in every child by the raincoat lapels and throws him into the greatest hits of children's fiction. Through the literary sampling and focusing of these classics, the immediate relevance to the life of the audience floods through, and the urge to grab a book is piqued.

As is the urge to imagine, and play, and adventure.

And the Weeblies are some of the funniest things I have ever seen on a stage.

I think one of the best testaments to a play is who wants to make it with you – it can sometimes be especially hard casting young people's work. But this one? Just send it to them, they'll call you back.

Read it with your children or on your own, make it with five pros or a whole class of youngsters.

It is a rollercoaster down memory lane and back via nail biting scrapes and death defying stunts.

An *Alice in Wonderland* for boys and book clubs.

Geoff Bullen

I recall the show *Chairperson* was a response to the 1981 United Nations International Year of Disabled Persons – how quaint that now sounds. The company that produced it was a substratum of Theatre Centre called Theatre Centre Islington, which was funded by the Urban Partnership. It was designed by Maz Bullen, and given a conscious 1950s storybook feel, to emphasise the infantile state in which Dudley was cocooned. We opened with breezy, chirrupy music and ended, as Dudley snatched off his uncool pullover and struggled into a well-cool t-shirt, with 'The Teardrop Explodes' 'Kilimanjaro' and 'When I Dream'.

The script was considerably worked at in rehearsal, so much so that it seemed we had only a few days to actually get it on – but at least we felt the script was sound. It was literally cut and paste in those days: and I remember happily gluing away while the marriage of Charles and Diana was announced.

We researched with disabled young people and their parents and did a lot of work with the fabulous Bert, now Sir Bert Massie.

www.disabilitynow.org.uk/article/sir-bert-massie-unrepentant-pragmatist

We did an excerpt at the Festival Hall for a Disability Conference and had to run the gauntlet of disabled campaigners, who disagreed with the event (I can't recall why, was it *Daily Mail* driven?) – and indeed an able-bodied actor playing Dudley would not now be considered PC, but Bert had no problems, as he felt the most important point we could make was that disabled pupils should attend normal schools. (He also praised Chris's performance for its physical accuracy.) We subsequently played to numerous disabled audiences with no problem: and I saw it once with a disabled actor, an Asian guy whose name I can't recall, though I remember he did stand-up – and his shtick was to let his crutches fall to the ground and say, "See! They're useless without me!"

Lin Coghlan

Bretevski Street began life as a completely different play.

I had been commissioned by Theatre Centre, the company that gave me my first commission, to write a play for 10–13 year olds on Irish myth and legend, an idea I had proposed.

I was some way along with it when one day I got off the train at London Bridge Station and saw a copy of a newspaper on a news stand with a photograph which made me stop in my tracks. It showed a close up image of a young boy inside a bus, tears streaming down his face, his hand pressed to the glass of the window, his father's hand pressed to the other side, as they said goodbye. It was 1993 and the bus was full of refugees leaving Yugoslavia in the midst of the war which had begun there two years earlier. It was an image of utter despair. I couldn't stop thinking about that boy. Where was he now? What had become of him? I remember being ten so clearly. What would it feel like to be so young and go through what he was experiencing?

I started to question why I was writing a story about Irish myth and legend when there was a war going on right on our doorstep. But I was intimidated by the subject matter. Had I any right to say anything about it, never having lived in Yugoslavia? I had never been a refugee. I had never lived through a war. It seemed like it might be easier not to go there. But I couldn't stop thinking about that boy. He was the same age as the target audience I was writing for, and the war that was raging was having a huge impact on children.

I went to Theatre Centre and told them how I felt. I was unsure of myself, of what I could do, or whether I had the right to do it. It is at a time such as this every writer longs for an act of faith from their commissioning company and that's exactly what I got. Theatre Centre told me to take a chance and see where it took me.

They supported my instinct to try to write about the world we were living in at that moment in time, they provided a safe and supportive environment in which to dare to see what might be done.

Writing now, so many years later, and having had the experience of working in many different media, I remain deeply grateful to have started my writing life with an organisation that always championed writers and supported them to take risks – and when I went on to work for Red Ladder, The Half Moon Young Peoples Theatre, Nottingham Roundabout, Clean Break, and many others, what I benefited from consistently was a family of like-minded practitioners who valued new voices and who weren't afraid to take chances. Without those companies I would never have become a writer.

In the end I decided to begin from what I knew – my childhood growing up in Dublin during the Troubles, being Catholic, being Irish, my family, their sense of identity, my country's history of invasion, rebellion and revolution.

That was something I could understand. I researched stories from other parts of the world, Germany in the Second World War, Eastern Europe, violence and prejudice in England, in London. Stories friends told me, documentaries, news stories, all went into the pot and I tried not to get overwhelmed.

The text began as a short piece which I didn't like much. I tried to create a fictitious place for the story to unfold but everyone who read it thought it was set in Ireland. Then it came to me that the heart of the story for me was much more about what any one of us might do if put under enough pressure rather than which particular country or culture should be the setting. We might all do terrible things if put in a terrible situation, perhaps that would be the most interesting story to tell for this young audience. Perhaps the people who did the 'terrible things', the people who sent that poor boy away on that bus, were people just like us?

I began by creating a street. A street just like my own. I would have people living in it much like the people who lived near me. They would have a mixture of traditions and names and music. They would have dreams and jealousies and pets and mothers, and games and songs and problems and one day a war would come.

This is how *Bretevski Street* began. It is made up but it's also a real place. It is our place. The play was produced by Theatre Centre in 1994, dramaturged and directed by Philip Osment, an inspirational mentor. Philip created a powerful production which elicited enthusiastic reactions in schools and communities. I was particularly moved by the way the children were interested in exploring the motives of all the characters, and the way they recognised that in a situation where a person's very survival is at risk, it is never a straightforward thing to judge their decisions. Those young audiences brought insight, curiosity and compassion to their debates about the nature of the human spirit under duress.

I still wonder about that boy on the bus. What happened to him? If he survived he would be about 30 now.

Neil Duffield

I don't think of writing for children and young people as being significantly different to writing for adults. My plays are essentially story-telling, with a beginning, a middle and an end, though not necessarily in that order. Deciding on the story and the best way to tell it are always my starting points, whatever the age of the audience. Obviously, adjustments have to be made, depending on the age of those watching, but I do believe it's possible to write plays that have meaning and appeal to a broad-based audience. *Talking with Angels* was advertised as being suitable 'for everyone over the age of seven', and I'd like to think that many of my plays fall into the same category. My aim is always to keep the audience engaged in the narrative, wondering what's going to happen next and identifying with the characters and the situations they find themselves in. I believe that children are capable of understanding and handling a full range of emotions, even involving (in the case of *Talking with Angels*) difficult concepts like war and death.

Kevin Dyer

In the old days, those of us in the TIE movement thought Children's Theatre was a dirty word (or two). Now the pendulum has swung the other way. Now children's theatre is a very broad artistic world using many media and having great strength in its diversity.

As TIE practitioners we used to think we were more political, more relevant somehow. Nowadays TIE and its issue-based work, its blatant educational approach, can seem so narrow, so doctrinal, so in the laps of the funders (health, drugs, police).

I've always tried to write the best plays I can that tell great stories of really interesting characters. I know I haven't always succeeded, of course, but I do believe that *all* plays have issues and themes (*King Lear*, the works of Mamet and Miller) and that audiences bring their own morality to a piece of literature. As such, it is a much better thing for an audience if the writer asks questions and leaves things unsaid. It is infinitely preferable if we set up situations on stage where there are dilemmas that someone in the audience can feel conflicted about – rather than saying; 'this is the answer'.

I do try to write plays about stuff that matters. It's like a photographer, isn't it? Take a photo of something that's dramatic or beautiful or surprising and you're off to a good start. So when I heard about Jo Berry, and how she had become friends with the man who killed her dad, I knew there was a story worth telling. I also knew this would be of interest to a young audience of course – because 'getting on' with people who are different to you is so important in school lives. I also try to write plays that I can take my parents and my friends to as well as my children – because they need drama too, to watch dangerous, thought-provoking and funny stuff and lose themselves for an hour.

And I'm interested in war – especially what is the effect of war on children. In *The Monster Under the Bed* the fact that the dad is on active service is hugely important in the family, in the boy's head.

And in *Baghdad Zoo* I want whoever sees the play to spend just a little while trying to understand what it's like being a child in a war zone.

It's my job as writer to write about the world we live in. It's my job as writer for young audiences to think of those audiences and the stories they would like to see. As such I'm not interested in writing the stories that I think they *should* see – that's a different thing. That's how I've escaped the TIE thing (of some bad work) of twenty-five years ago.

What frustrates me is that many of the plays older children see are connected to their education; the schools pay for adaptations of Shakespeare because there is going to be an exam on it. That's not a great use of actors and directors and designers, and I feel teaching children that theatre is there to support the curriculum is a reductive idea. Much better to tell new stories, fresh stories, and show visual theatricality, because it is delightful and amazing and full of inspiration.

In *Angel* I had no idea in the beginning that I was going to write a play about Miriam's dementia. In fact it isn't a play about dementia, rather it's a play about a woman who happens to have dementia. To her, finding her key and feeling safe and having a laugh are the important things – so that is what the play is about. And oddly, as I wrote it, the play became more about Bill – a young girl whose mum and dad are splitting up. It's a rights-of-passage play – as all plays are I suppose. Miriam is going through one as she 'loses her marbles' and so is the girl – not only as she physically changes, but also as she learns what her family is becoming and her life will be like without her dad.

In the 21st century we spend a lot of time in front of screens – watching films and videos and recorded drama. I love doing this, but I know it's different to theatre. Theatre is live in front of our eyes and it does things which film and TV can't do.

I get very bored with theatre plays that would work better on screen – so I try to write stuff that is not filmable. This means audiences get something in that live space that they could never ever get at home or in a cinema. That seems a worthwhile ambition.

Anthony Haddon

So many playwrights were born, cut their teeth and then emerged from the devising processes that Theatre in Education companies in the UK used to create plays. The democracy of creating a play together in a rehearsal room was seen as a significant challenge to the traditional, hierarchical structure of creating theatre and one that could be handed on to the children in schools who were offered the opportunity to take part and affect the course of the narrative events. Was this just an ideal? Did it create good art? Did the children really have any power to affect the process? Was there always a secret playwright in the devising company?

Well, all I can say is that Mike Kenny emerged from a very vibrant and successful devising team at Leeds Theatre in Education Company and found himself in the role of directing a play called *Bag Dancing* for the Theatre Company Blah Blah Blah. We were the new generation, in our early twenties, eager to learn from Mike's experience and follow his lead. We didn't know what the play was going to be about other than we were interested in exploring 'secrets and lies'. That was a vague starting point, which we explored in all sorts of ways until it became clear to Mike that he just needed to shut himself away and write it. This play marks the launching of Mike's career as a playwright and the evolution of the Blahs' theatre making DNA.

Vicky Ireland

I was raised in a small family hotel which my parents ran, in Scarborough, on the North East coast of Yorkshire and I trained at the Central School of Speech and Drama in London.

Just before graduating in June 1966, I was informed that my college had put me up for a job, to join the newly formed Theatre in Education team at the Belgrade Theatre, Coventry. I duly went along, did auditions over a weekend, got the job and started that September as the youngest member of the seven-strong team. I learnt so much from this extraordinary start, and it was to influence the rest of my working life. It was a huge privilege to be part of the TIE movement which has influenced British theatre in so many positive ways, principally being responsible for the creation of great plays for young audiences which tackle big questions; of talking to young people with respect and encouraging their involvement; discussing difficult subjects whilst being politically aware; tackling disability; using integrated casting; making the audience feel they own the play and allowing them to learn about so many aspects of what it is to be human…

I also met Paul Harman at Belgrade TIE, and we have been friends and working colleagues ever since. My other great friend, who joined the team and from whom I learnt so much, was Stuart Bennett – like me, a Scarborian.

I went on to work in TIE and as an actress in reps all over Britain and also presented for twelve years, BBC's TV's educational programme, *Words and Pictures*. I wrote for Radio and TV, including in 1989, the BBC *Happy Families* series, based on the books by Allan Ahlberg. The first play, originally commissioned by Quicksilver Theatre brought with it the casting diversity we had used in TIE from its conception. The series was labelled 'A rare example of integrated casting'. Little or no recognition, then or since, has been given to the TIE movement for understanding so early on, the need to

reflect and empower our audiences in all their ethnic richness. Something adult theatre is just trying to come to terms with.

From 1988–2000, I was artistic Director of Polka Theatre which included the commissioning of new plays and putting talented artists together to create productions. I had a wide palette of subjects to draw upon and I came to work alongside a range of wonderfully talented theatre writers, and authors including Alan Ayckbourn, David Holman, Charles Way, Mike Kenny, Neil Duffield, Brendan Murray, Richard Pinner, David Tse, Alan Ahlberg, Lynne Reid Banks, Philip Pullman, Malorie Blackman, Jamila Gavin and Beverley Naidoo.

In 2001 we created the appointment of Director of New Writing, the first Literary Manager for Theatre for Children.

Some years later, I heard Martin Drury, former Artistic Director of The Ark in Dublin, say, "Running a children's theatre is like running a small family hotel", and those dolphins rose from the water in the famous synchronicity picture as I realised my upbringing was very apt for the position I so relished.

The charity, Action for Children's Arts was started at Polka in 1989 with David Wood as Chair and myself as Vice Chair, out of a need to reach out across art forms to make the voice for children's arts stronger. Situations have improved, but still too many of us are waiting to be asked to sit at artistic tables, where representation for children is nil.

ASSITEJ, the International Association of Theatre for Children and Young People, has played a large part in my life. Like Paul, I sat on the International Executive to represent the UK and held the position of Treasurer.

As with integrated casting, the subjects of inclusivity and difference have always been present in our work, and in 2014 it was with great pride that I joined with Daryl Beeton and other world Inclusivity champions to be part of the working group which created IIAN, The International Inclusive Arts Network, the newest branch of ASSITEJ.

In Japan, the crane symbolises long life, good health and peace. In 2006, the performer Kumiko Mendl and I founded, A Thousand Cranes, a company which seeks to bridge East and West, by sharing the stories, traditions and art forms of Japan with young audiences.

This year is our tenth birthday and we have just started working on a new show.

When I was twelve, a lady came to work as my father's secretary and her teenage son Alan visited her, and talked to me as we both hung about the hotel. Some years later, I worked for him – the famous Alan Ayckbourn – in BBC Radio North plays and also at The Theatre Royal, York.

Our friendship has lasted ever since and this year, 2016, I return to Scarborough to dramatize and direct *The Just So Stories* by Rudyard Kipling as the summer family show at The Stephen Joseph Theatre.

In 2016, I celebrate my 50th year of working in TIE/TYA. It remains as inspiring and challenging as ever.

Mike Kenny

I'm not sure that Theatre in Education still exists in the way I understood it. These days I'm more likely to hear it mentioned in dismissive tones. TIE has become synonymous with didactic and un-theatrical, un-dramatic, and all round piss poor. It used to be the opposite of that. It hit me personally like a runaway train, or a Damascene conversion and I knew I had to do it. That was 1972/3 and I was in my first year at college, training to be a teacher in Birmingham. I saw a lecture demo of Coventry Belgrade TIE, and that was that. Love. It was the circus, and I had to run away with it.

It wasn't until I'd finished my degree and got some experience under my belt that I actually managed to get a job with Leeds Playhouse TIE at the start of 1978.

TIE came out of a time where theatre was becoming more democratised and education more child-centred. TIE always seemed to have a very simple principle at its heart. If children can't or won't go to the theatre, then take the theatre to them.

This simple pebble of an idea had ripples which are still felt. It changed theatre itself. Firstly, it affected the company makeup.

If you are actually in a room with your audience, and you can see not just the whites of their eyes, but all of them, then you start to think that you should in some way reflect them. I came in at the end of the first wave of this, the arrival of working class actors, closely followed by many more women. This opened up to BAME actors, LGBT actors and disabled performers.

The resulting clamour of diverse voices affected the subject matters tackled. Different companies had differing obsessions and artistic voices. The Leeds Company that I was in was constantly fascinated by the fall out of Empire, and the unheard voices of women, working class and ethnic minority histories. We were also sensitive to the times we were living through.

Raj came out of the inner city riots, *Flags and Bandages*, set in the Crimean War, was as much influenced by the Falklands war. Some pieces were set in the streets and playgrounds of Leeds. I remember companies on the other side of the Pennines exploring links to the cotton trade and slavery. Coventry Belgrade seemed to be fascinated by emigration and immigration.

In the same way that I saw culturally mixed companies for the first time in school halls, I saw issues of race, gender and sexual orientation tackled for the first time too.

The first plays that looked at hot topics like nuclear armament, the environment, the troubles in Northern Ireland, were all first done by TIE companies.

From the start, from the world of education, one of the biggest explorations was in theatrical form. An acting space was as likely to be in the round, or traverse. A play could be in many parts, it could happen in various locations all over the school and sometimes outside, on buses, barges, playgrounds and streets.

And there was often the active participation of the audiences. These days immersion is being explored by young companies. I have yet to see it done as dangerously, or as riskily as it was done with infant school children in the Belgrade's *Pow Wow*. Years later, again at the Belgrade, in *Landrush*, I found myself in a log cabin with an actor, who within the story had apparently been poisoned and was lying unconscious on the floor, and a class of 7-year olds falling back on their own resources to discuss the best thing to do. They were totally bound up in the narrative and didn't turn to the adults to sort it out.

TIE has clearly changed, but then so has everything else. Theatre is no longer democratic. Ensembles have pretty much disappeared, and actors are expected to serve the text and the director, rather than be creative in their own right. Education is target-driven.

Chippy actors encouraging lively debate are no longer welcome in an education system which became wedded to the measurable, the testable, the controllable. I don't know where feeling and imagination fit in. I was outraged by TIE's demise and still am. I saw some of the most gut-wrenching, life-changing theatre in schools.

What It Means to Work With Learning Disabled People

It's shocking how we can take some things for granted until our attention is drawn to them. It's an even bigger leap to do something about it. Some doors seem to be locked that aren't. They just have the weight of history leaning against them, which makes them resistant to opening.

When I first entered theatre in the 70s I came through a recently opened door with a passion for making work for those who had little voice. I'd grown up working class on a rural council estate and saw myself as one of those excluded. Much of my first ten years was spent in working with the clamouring voices of class, race, gender and sexual orientation which came flooding out of the 70s and 80s.

Towards the end of that time I was working on a play about disability. None of the cast were disabled. We were serious and impassioned and researched and interviewed many people, both disabled and non-disabled. Then one day, a guy I was talking to who had cerebral palsy said to me, 'Why am I not in this play?' It's a damn good question. It's one that bears repeating. Years ago Sheila Rowbotham said, the task is to make the door wider. I'd add to that now that some people may need a ramp and a bit of a hand up, but it's still the same task.

Learning disabled people have had to wait a long time before they got to tell their own stories on the stages of the world. I've been involved in ways of helping them do it since I arrived at Mind the Gap, and it has been an adventure for all of us.

This work is truly ground-breaking, and throws down a gauntlet to mainstream work. I'm not sure the gauntlet is being taken up yet, though the mainstream has started to take note. This kind of thing is a step in the right direction for equal opportunities, though I think it won't much affect our continued adventures at Mind the Gap.

We will still be posing questions and leaning on doors, heaving them open, and I will be very proud to be involved.

Philip Osment

I first started writing plays for young audiences in 1989 when I was introduced to the work of Red Ladder and Theatre Centre by my friend Noël Greig.

My work for young people was inspired by a desire to address situations, concerns and problems that I faced myself as a child and as a teenager. As a gay person growing up in North Devon in the 1960s I was painfully aware of the sense of isolation that young people can feel at times of crisis and all of my plays have explored such situations in the hope that, on the one hand, audience members who are facing similar problems will realise that they are not alone and will derive a sense of hope and perspective that will help them move on into adult life; and, on the other hand, that audience members who might not understand such problems or might even have attitudes that exacerbate the problem will develop empathy and change their attitudes accordingly.

Whole was commissioned by the pioneering theatre company 20 Stories High whose commitment to exploring form and addressing the concerns of young people today was a huge inspiration.

Richard Pinner

Rosie Blitz proved to be a real watershed in my career, receiving excellent national and metropolitan reviews and awards. It was commissioned as the first new play that Vicky Ireland produced at Polka Theatre, in her distinguished career there as Artistic Director. And it emerged from our previous happy collaboration, as co-writers, on Radio 4's innovative children's drama series, *Cliffhanger.*

Having lived in both the East End and the shires of Northamptonshire I readily conceived of the locations of action for my story. But the real breakthrough I made in theatrical style came about through my research – firstly into the great English tradition of playground and street songs, and then the East End's hybrid vernacular – which provided me with such a richly textured milieu for this play.

John Retallack

During the period that I was artistic director of Oxford Stage Company (1989–1999) I won an Arts Council bursary to go and see theatre for children and young people in France, Holland, Italy and Germany. In Holland I went to the Den Bosch Festival and it opened up a new world for me.

The work was inspirational. Content was contemporary with a clear political awareness; the acting companies were strong and well-versed in ensemble technique and spirit; viewed simply as theatre it was ravishing – yet shows took place in school gymnasiums in daylight. The work was strikingly sophisticated and assertively modern in delivery because it had a clear purpose – to intrigue and to entertain young audiences who would soon be citizens with a vote to cast and a role to play in the world. These performances surpassed the drab surroundings in which they were placed and gained an almost transcendental theatrical power in doing so. At the time of one performance, Wederzijd's production of *Hitler's Childhood.*, I wrote:

> "Adults know much about the end of Hitler, but who knows about the beginning? Is a fascist dictator born evil or is he made evil? These are pertinent questions in a part of Belgium where the Vlaams Blok is winning so many votes. This performance was accurately judged and conceived with great imagination and intelligence. It was also very beautiful to look at and to listen to. It was the most original work I've seen all year. It makes theatre for young people a fresh prospect and makes me speculate if it might be an exciting step to take personally."

Oxford Stage Company and Wederzijds worked together frequently between 1993 and 1998 and the relationship with its artistic leader, Ad de Bont continues still. It was Ad de Bont's work that introduced me to the same perfectionist aesthetic that I was familiar with from growing up and competing in a theatre world whose standards in England were set – for me – by Mike Alfred's Shared Experience, Theatre de Complicité, Cheek by Jowl, Deborah Warner's Kick Theatre Company and in France and Germany by Ariane Mnouchkine, Peter Brook and Peter Stein – these were my lasting formative influences. ATC (8 years) and Oxford Stage Company (10 years) were shaped by watching the work of these companies and in meeting and knowing the directors in question. They were my 'gold standard'.

From the time that my own two children, Hanna and Jack, were born in the mid-80s, I became more interested in work for children and young people. I asked myself; "If children's books are so good, why are they not matched by a similar achievement in the performing arts?"

Funding was low and there was clearly limited respect for this genre – and it showed. All the brilliant companies that I mention above played overseas and were known in Europe – but an English company at a young people's theatre festival in Europe was a very rare sighting. They were simply not on anyone's list. English acting for children frustrated me – it seemed both over-energized and bored at the same time. It also seemed a place that actors really didn't want to be.

My surprise in discovering the work of Wederzijds and several other companies in Holland was that these companies were clearly working to their own 'gold standard'. This was, for me, an undiscovered theatre world as exacting and aspiring as the one that shaped me. I am a trained teacher and an untrained theatre director. The discovery of the 'perfectionist' aesthetic in the domain of theatre for young people linked worlds that I thought had no connection.

I wrote *Hannah and Hanna* after running a few workshops for teenagers in and around Margate. At the time I wrote the play, teenagers in schools in Britain were told very little about why large groups of people from other countries arrived overnight. All they knew is that they were asylum-seekers, people from nowhere.

National and local community leaders show little interest in 'introducing' these strangers to the local community.

In school classrooms, pupils sometimes did not know where the boy or girl in the next desk was actually from. That's hard for those who turn up here and hard on the local people who don't know why they're at the bus stop, in the waiting room at the dentists or slowing up the queue at the supermarket check-out. In small towns, the reaction to asylum-seekers could be more violent, not less. In Margate, in 2000, there was an overnight dumping of hundreds of Kosovans. The town could talk of little else; pensioners were outraged, teenagers declared war, the local newspapers had a story that would run and run.

How could a local Margate teenager – in that climate – ever meet, let alone *befriend*, a Kosovan teenager who'd survived the invasion of her country and ended up in Margate? And at what point, supposing that a friendship did develop, would the two girls open up to each other? Were there any circumstances that could bring about a real and unprompted exchange between them?

I wanted to acknowledge the role of us, the British audience, in the drama of the refugee. 'We' are the hosts who determine the fate of such people, our guests. 'We' are central characters, not onlookers and outsiders. To the asylum-seekers, 'we' are the main players. That's why I started with two teenagers who mimic the attitudes of their parents, yet, unlike their parents, they still have time to change their minds.

Hannah and Hanna is a strong narrative and it has struck a nerve in many places. It is playing now in France, Germany, Holland and Portugal and it has been seen in several countries beyond Europe.

Hannah and Hanna is often performed in schools; once I saw twelve Hanna/hs do a 'relay' performance of the play. It can be performed with almost no props or set whatsoever (this happened twice on tour when the set failed to arrive). What it does require is real physical movement and dance.

Peter Rumney

Cosmos and *Jumping on my Shadow* represent themes which appear again and again in my writing – loss and dislocation. They also seem to be about the telling of stories. Every child has a story to tell, but all too often they are patronised by adults who aren't interested in listening. I believe passionately that children are capable of, indeed, need to grapple with powerful themes and big ideas. I am very much inspired by visual narrative, spatial design and music, and by the collaborators who help to generate the spoken text. But, above all, everything I write is drawn from and reflects, I hope, the voices of children.

Nona Shepphard

They say that 'Necessity is the mother of Invention' and I always found this saying totally appropriate when working in YPT; the constraints of small companies, limited set and costume budgets and touring to venues such as carpeted school halls, plus the need to have clarity and theatrical excitement, always made me ambitious to produce work that would enthral and challenge young audiences.

Roy Williams

I started out in Young People's Theatre. It is where I found my love for the arts and my voice for writing. Young People's Theatre made me feel inclusive regardless of who I was and where I came from. I will continue to write for young audiences because it is my way of helping to keep it alive, to encourage the next generation to fall in love with the arts as I did. To allow themselves to be pushed and challenged and to always ask hard questions of themselves and of the world they are living in. To never be dismissed.

Charles Way

I turned 60 in 2015, so I began writing professionally almost forty years ago. This hardly seems believable but it's true. It's also true that writing plays for children and young people hasn't got any easier and I still suffer from the same old doubts which are part and parcel of a creative life. It is also true that I still feel my best work is yet to come. This may be delusional but it spurs me on. Lyn Gardner of the *Guardian* said in a preview to a play of mine that I would be better known if I had not written most of my plays for children and community audiences. This is probably true – though being well-known has never been much of a drive, which causes me to ask what it is I have wanted to achieve. I think the answer lies in the creative nature of childhood (my own included) and also watching children across the world have to live the hardships that others, namely adults, offer up to them in the name of their own ideologies.

Writing 'for' children does give one a sense that it is not a solipsistic exercise and that it has a social purpose. Due to my early political education this has always felt important. It can however lead one to 'preach' to children and this is something one must never do. Children themselves, their joys and sorrows, spur me on to create plays which are I hope entertaining, but also have a strong whiff of emotional truth so that the child is never 'spoken down to'.

Our creative lives as adults come from our childhood experiences and I feel this strongly for myself and have a desire to address the adult world with this reality. We have a duty of care – to give to the young, artistic experiences and opportunities which open doors in their emotional and intellectual lives. It has never been more important to feel what it is like to be in 'someone else's shoes' and theatre/drama is perhaps the ideal form. In my artistic life there has been nothing more rewarding than sitting at the back of an audience of young people either in a school or a theatre and witnessing their engagement – in itself so full of desire and hope to be part of the world – and to be able to talk to them afterwards about the nature of their experience. Sometimes they literally sit wide-eyed, able to take in and understand far more than their teachers or parents give them credit for.

A writer is, as a natural consequence of the profession, a bit of a lone wolf but I have always created work with theatres or companies and I would like to stress the importance of other people in my creative process and in doing so the importance of what we used to call 'the young people's theatre movement'. It was from this 'sector' that playwrights wanting to write for young audiences emerged, many of whom had been actors or directors. It meant that the scripts were generally based in the physical reality of the 'empty space' and that the craft of playwriting could be practised with actors, designers and directors close at hand in companies such as Leeds TIE, York YPT, Gwent Theatre, Theatre Powys, etc.

Many of these companies have now been axed and schools' touring has not only suffered but virtually disappeared so that many children in Shakespeare's land will never get to see a play. At present the arts are directed toward those who in their lucky childhoods were introduced to the arts and who can now afford to drive to the theatre or perhaps to a remote setting for a theatre installation and then have a pizza, etc. ...

The divide between rich and poor has never been greater across the globe and this is reflected in the way that theatre has become divorced from the common experience. It is reflected in children's theatre in Britain. In the whole of Britain there are only three building-based companies specifically dedicated to children's theatre and those companies who did take theatre into schools have largely been cut.

Time for a re-think?

ADAPTATIONS: WHY AND HOW?

VICKY IRELAND

When I became Artistic Director at Polka Theatre, I started to programme book adaptations as I wanted a rich mix of new writing, versions of well-known traditional stories, adaptations of classic books and modern authors' work for our young audience. I also had the opportunity to direct many of the adaptations which allowed me a complete vision of a production, from page to stage.

My starting points were very varied. For example, I commissioned Greg Lyons to adapt *The Starlight Cloak* by Jenny Nimmo, an Irish version of *Cinderella*, after being totally inspired by the performance of the Irish dance routine in *Riverdance* and wanting a show that had marvellous traditional Irish dancing and music in it.

Whilst looking for role models for children, I was so impressed by hearing the profoundly deaf percussionist Evelyn Glennie on BBC Radio's *Desert Island Discs*, that I got in touch with her and she allowed me to commission Charles Way to write his beautiful play based on her biography, *Good Vibrations*. She also visited rehearsals and helped us in a hundred ways.

Sometimes it was my complete love of a certain classic book such as *Beowulf*, which was adapted into a brilliant play, or *The Borrowers*, adapted by Charles Way, or *The House at Pooh Corner* and *The Secret Garden*, both adapted by Neil Duffield. For the dramatisation of *The Diary of Anne Frank*, I had to be interviewed by the Anne Frank foundation to ensure my reasons for creating a new version would honour her memory, and I'm glad to say the resulting play, *Dreams of Anne Frank* by Bernard Kops is a remarkable piece and has been produced all around the world.

I also wanted to share other cultures, and to this end asked the author Jamila Gavin to adapt her book, *Monkey in the Stars* which tells the story of the Hindu festival, Diwali and she also wrote her own dramatization of Rudyard Kipling's, *Just So Stories*. I was very proud of the adaptation by Michael Miller of *The Patchwork Quilt* by Valerie Flournoy, the story of a loving African-American family and their quilt, which in turn led to the school audiences who visited, each bringing a patchwork square they had made, to be part of one beautiful new Polka quilt, full of memories.

One of my own adaptations was prompted by the 100th anniversary of *The Jungle Book* in 1994. Another, *The Last Noo-Noo*, by Jill Murphy because I just love the book. Likewise I love the daft gentle fun of *The Giraffe and the Pelly and Me* by Roald Dahl which I adapted into a musical play, and the wonderfully emotional roller-coaster of *Kensuke's Kingdom* by Michael Morpurgo, which remains one of my favourite pieces.

Occasionally it works the other way round and it was intriguing when Polka plays were turned into books, which is what happened to Alan Ahlberg's play *The Giant's Baby* and David Tse's play of the Chinese tale *The Magic Paintbrush*.

As Artistic Director it was a great privilege to make my own choices of what to adapt and why, but one of the biggest influences on my decisions was the Polka Children's Council, which I set up as a sounding board for everything the theatre was trying to achieve. This group of children from 6-12 years talked regularly to me about the books they loved, the TV programmes they watched and what they enjoyed about theatre. One small girl recommended the poems of Alan Ahlberg and this led to two of my happiest shows. I adapted his two books of school poems, *Please Mrs Butler* and *Heard it in the Playground* to create the musical play *Three Cheers for Mrs Butler*, and his book of football poems into the musical play Friendly Matches. I also adapted twelve of his *Happy Family* books for BBC Children's TV.

Another gift the Children's Council gave me was to introduce me to a writer I hadn't heard of at the time – Jacqueline Wilson. Their enthusiasm was such that after persuading me to read one of her books, I got in touch with her agent and in 1999, I adapted her book *The Lottie Project,* which was such a runaway success, that I followed it with *Double Act, Bad Girls, The Suitcase Kid, Midnight* and *Secrets* which all toured the UK. It was an introduction by a young person to a very much loved children's author, which resulted in many happy years of collaboration. I say this as I believe children are full of brilliant ideas and we should talk and listen to them more.

At the start of the process, whether adapting myself or commissioning another playwright, I have to choose a book I believe in, by which I mean it will have a lasting effect, be relevant and touch the children both intellectually and emotionally. I need to decide that it will work in the different medium of theatre, that is has a strong story and interesting characters. If the scope is huge, I have to think how to handle this with usually only a small cast; if puppets or video projection might be included; if I need the skills of a choreographer or a circus artist. Often exciting physical movement and dance can move the story on just as much as text.

I then approach the author's agent to acquire the rights for the book and their permission to adapt it into a play, giving details of the proposed production. Once permission has been granted, and royalty fees agreed, I assemble the creative team and hold a workshop to share ideas. This will involve some workshop actors, the designer and composer, and often, the author. Usually authors are very keen to attend and enjoy the process of discussing dramatization ideas. I make sure they feel welcome and they are invited to observe rehearsals. I respect their observations and recommendations whilst encouraging them to be brave and trust in the process, as we make sure we cross the bridge from book to play.

Alan Ahlberg was the exception. The dearest and kindest of men, he never attended rehearsals or even saw the plays, he was so nervous that he might not like them. The same applied to all TV adaptations of his books. On the other hand, Lynne Reid Banks so loved the process that she would have camped in the rehearsal room.

I bring to the workshop my initial ideas on how the book can be staged and what I think would be dramatically exciting. I have to get to know the book which takes time. It feels a bit like walking round and round a locked house in the dark and then suddenly finding a way to break in, and once inside, feeling at home. The same with the characters. I need to get to know how they tick, so I can feel confident about projecting them.

Once I'm inside the story, the nuts and bolts of the process are; to précis the action, decide how much I can include and what I need to cut; that the play has a dramatic arc; where to place the interval if there is to be one; where physicality and dance, music and songs might be appropriate; how to solve impossible questions such as travelling through the air, swimming under the sea; if the actors play more than one role, making sure they have time to change between characters.

I try to keep as close as possible to the original novel as I appreciate most authors have thought about every word they write, about every incident, and most importantly, the shape of their story. Who am I to interfere with this? Plus in my experience, children get very cross when books they know and love are changed, as they don't understand why. The bottom line for me is that the play must work for the children. A battered copy of the book is kept in rehearsals for referral.

I often have actors in mind for the roles, as once one has found a good character actor with a real sense of humour who is prepared and willing to perform for children, you hold onto them. They are gold-dust. Likewise, the designers, lighting designers and composers who are intuitive and empathetic to your way of working.

Sound for me is crucial and songs and music that capture important moments can really lift and expand the story. In *The Jungle Book*, we put in Kipling's story, *How Fear Came*, and Neil Brand wrote the most brilliant score which the actors sang.

Lighting too plays a really important part. In Jacqueline Wilson's *Bad Girls*, each chapter of the book is connected with a different colour, both in the action, the words and the objects. This is a very subtle and interesting take and one we used in the play's scenes, mainly through lighting, with the lights eventually building into a rainbow at the story's finale.

Sometimes the pictures in a book are crucial to its personality and story-telling as with *The Last Noo-Noo* by Jill Murphy and we had great fun copying the look of her characters and creating a huge Noo-Noo tree at the end. I think younger children love that recognition and enjoy seeing well-loved characters and scenes brought alive on stage, as if they've just stepped out of the book.

If the story has impossible technical demands, I don't avoid them but instead, put them in the script and see if others with more knowledge can solve them. In Michael Morpurgo's Kensuke's Kingdom, I wrote the stage direction for a tropical downpour, and to my delight, pipes were put in place high above the stage, water was pumped, troughs were installed and on cue, a tropical downpour magically happened all around the acting area. *In Three Cheers for Mrs Butler* the cast had a visit to a swimming pool, so the designer, Bridget Kimak invented cartoon bathing costumes to hide adult bodies, and made a deep trench in the stage, which when needed, became a very realistic pool.

If there's a will, there's often a very theatrical way, supplied by your team.

Characters can sometimes be challenging. In *The Lottie Project*, one of the main characters is a seven year old boy. The author Jacqueline Wilson was very keen that it should not be a puppet child or a small girl, – which might have been possible solutions, – so to honour her feelings, I held auditions and two small boys, plus chaperones, took it in turns to share the part. Likewise, *Double Act* involved twins, but after much searching, I managed to find two excellent look-alike actresses, and once they had similar wigs, they absolutely were twins on stage.

Once a script was been written it may be polished by a further production with slight changes, but usually the main change is when one is requested to reduce a two act play to one act. Growing a one act play into two acts is far harder.

If you are thinking of adapting, make sure you care deeply about your chosen book, that you have a theatrical style in mind to support telling its story, and that you have permission from the author's agent.

Finally, making theatre is team work. The script is just one element and the production can be influenced and helped on its way by all those involved. When it comes together, alongside the author, we all share the agony, the ecstasy and the credits.

TV Adaptations for Young Audiences

If children see a TV show on stage, it's usually very similar to the screen version. This is because TV producers keep hold of their artistic vision and want to ensure good sales of both tickets and merchandise. If the artistic vision is handed over to the theatre-makers they will create a very different product often with much more of an aesthetic heart, but also a more risky one as it may not be what the adult punters are expecting or want.

Artistic values are sometimes overlooked by adults who are convinced their child shouting and eating sweets and being hyper for two hours is the manifestation of enjoyment and proof of the show's success. A quiet thoughtful reception is often deemed as failing to please.

When a good piece of theatre hits home, it is an artform, not in competition with TV but an entirely different experience. It is about being live and creating an engagement between performers and audience which is of the moment and subject to change. In this way, the child is drawn into the action in a completely different and powerful way and this can be very pleasing for them.

Good theatre is memorable. It offers the opportunity for dialogue, the exchange of opinions and the start of critical appreciation. It is also very potent and can upset and frighten. We need to challenge young audiences with our work, but be responsible about how we do this.

Children under five in the UK spend roughly a year of their lives watching television. I feel it is important to offer them the best of theatre alongside the best of television to share with their families.

Good Examples

Well-known adaptations worthy of mention are: *The Railway Children* by Mike Kenny, *Matilda* by Dennis Kelly (Book) and Tim Minchin (Music and Lyrics), *Goodnight Mr Tom* and *The Tiger Who Came to Tea* by David Wood, *The Borrowers* by Charles Way, *The Secret Garden* by Neil Duffield, and *The Gruffalo* adapted for Tall Stories.

Notes from a Forum held in 2005 during the 15th ASSITEJ Congress and General Assembly in Montreal

A fruitful session was held where the subject of adaptation was discussed. Many good questions were raised:

> "How do you find the original heartbeat of the story? What are the pulse, the tone of the original and how do you find and use that in concert with your own creativity?"
>
> US playwright Susan Zeder.

What are:

a) The differences and similarities between inter-cultural and intra-cultural adaptations,

b) The differences between editing, adapting and creating a new piece of art,

c) The main differences between, and requirement of, a piece of literature and a theatrical production?

The commercial aspect of adapting children's literature to theatre; we are often tempted to use popular literature because it 'sells well'.

The moral issues in the use of 'diary' theatre; do we have the right to edit and adapt real, personal experiences?

Who has ownership of the work and who is the best person to adapt; the original writer or a theatre practitioner, or a collaboration of both?

We should remember that some books are well known and liked by children; how much right do we have, therefore, to change them into something totally new?

What does the book mean to us, now, here, today? What is the underlying thought?

The Two Extremes of the Argument

In summary, writers were divided into two camps which can be encapsulated by the differing views of myself and director Tony Graham:

> "In adapting we need to absorb the book, look for the essence and "throw the book out of the window" in order to create something new. The public's expectations of a book are sometimes our worst enemy in that they restrict our work."
>
> Tony Graham

> "Authors have ownership of their book and their ideas – we should respect this or not use the book at all. If you want to re-write it that much, you should write your own, or say 'based' on the book… Also, children love the details in books written for them; they can become upset and annoyed if we adults mess about and recreate the book in an unrecognisable form."
>
> Vicky Ireland

ACTING LIKE CHILDREN
NINA HAJIYIANNI & KEVIN DYER

Play texts have to be acted. In 2011 three of the UK's leading theatre companies for children and young people, Travelling Light, Polka Theatre and Action Transport Theatre ran three open workshops.

In our sector of work we often have stories with child protagonists. This allows children in our audiences to see children like themselves as active, central figures in adventures. It also allows the stories to deal with the stuff of children's lives. Thus stories for children (in written fiction or plays) are often about two lots of children – the children in the story, and the children in the audience. In theatre, we have used adults to play these core characters in our plays for many years. We should try to portray them as well as we possibly can.

Why Use Adults to Play Children?

1. Habit – maybe we've been doing it for many years and know how to implement it in our working practices, so just carry on. It is true that children are being used more often in 'professional work' in current British Theatre – and not just in youth theatre and community or participatory projects – but this is still very much the exception.

2. Practicality – it is hard to tour with children; they are often in school, and touring with a child also means touring with a chaperone. Adult actors can get themselves to and from rehearsals and are, usually, lower 'maintenance'.

3. Cost – chaperones; two children to play one character is sometimes required; children can rehearse for less hours a day by law than an adult actor; licenses; all can make it more expensive than using an adult Equity member.

4. Acting skills – adult actors have been to drama school; they have vocal and physical characterisation skills that a child usually does not possess.

5. Adult actors can take on big parts, do stage combat, be in plays of an emotional nature or with a subject matter that we might feel uncomfortable asking a child to be in. Professional actors have rehearsal room 'savvy' and they can take direction. I say this even though the task of 'playing children' isn't 'core syllabus' in most UK drama schools. It is also clear that some actors simply cannot play children convincingly.

6. Less 'alienating'. Sometimes when we see a child on stage, we only see the child, not the character – it can be like nudity or extreme violence; it can take us out of the play. This seems a contradiction, but is sometimes true. The 'truth' can take us out of the world of pretend we have contracted into and the performance has created and maintained. On the other hand we do know that 'real children' can posses a quality ('truth'?) that a grown-up has lost.

The driving reason behind the three ALC workshops was to learn how we can do 'adult actors playing children' better. It was an attempt to bring some people together who have experience of this way of working and who could share a bit of wisdom – or at least ask a few incisive questions. It was also an opportunity for the lead companies to learn too – from each other and by giving time to something we do but rarely have the opportunity to analyse and work on outside the rehearsal room. It is a fact that in the rehearsal room we are often too busy getting the play on to consider this core element of our work.

We shared experiences as directors, producers and actors; watched both professional actors and children playing children; played as children ourselves; tried to pin down a few things that would help in future practice; tried to recognise some of the things we take for granted; tried to draw up some simple guidelines and conclusions.

One big question that recurred – sub-textually if not overtly – was this: if this is a core part of our work – adults playing characters much younger than themselves – why do we so often see it done so badly, and what are the things about these bad performances that we dislike? What are the secrets of those actors who do it well that we can share?

These are our key thoughts from the three days.

1. Some Exercises That Directors Use:

a)   Getting actors to watch children in their own family or that are in their friend's families

b)   Watching videos of children

c)   Closely examining photos of children

d)   Going into character using all the above; empathising with the above; compiling lists of the needs, wants concerns and feelings of observed children

e)   Going into schools and meeting children

f)   Listening to and playing games with children

g)   Working with children in drama groups and other sessions where children are 'themselves'

h)   Recalling your own childhood

i)   Listening to others talk about their childhood – and then playing that back as narrative or 'in character' or in any other way (drawing, sculpting, dancing etc., etc.)

j)   Look for clues in the text about language, action and aspirations

k)   Play as children – using any object – over extended periods (a training method used at the Jacques Lecoq theatre school in Paris)

l)   Use physical play to be children from birth to teenage years – pay special attention to the use of the spine

m) Play with the development of language – both sounds and words – from birth to adulthood

2. Some 'Do's':

a) Be yourself

b) Think about 'the child in yourself'

c) Be the child, not 'like a child'

d) Remember that all children are different. A child character is one child not all children.

e) Be specific not generic.

f) Find the Internal feelings and wants of the character – more important than making the character from the outside

g) Work on the character like you would any other character – use method or Stanislavsky or whatever your approach normally is – because child characters are essentially the same as any other.

h) Once you have found the character – forget about acting like a child.

i) Let the context of the story, situation, world do the work in placing the character. It may be best to do very little by way of 'showing'

j) Let emotional truth be your guiding star.

k) Be in each moment

We often use the term 'child-like' in relation to some of the qualities above as distinct from the idea of being 'childish', which seems to suggest behaviour, which is 'silly'. The former suggests a sense of genuine curiosity, the latter when someone acts deliberately younger than his or her age.

3. Some 'Don'ts':

a) Don't fidget and do externalities.

b) Don't do clichés and stereotypes like twizzling one leg or putting sellotape on your glasses or sucking your thumb or twisting your hair round your finger – unless you need to do comic stereotype. It is clear that part of the conditioning that comes on when we become adults is to control or wall in our physicality, but this is not to say that children are fidgeting all the time. This is the thing that most watchers of adults playing children hate. Saying that, some degree of physicality – a physical 'freedom' – is accepted and often welcomed by audiences. Especially with younger children, their tics and physical patterning can be very extreme. If these are imitated they can be ridiculous.

Maybe this is because the adult actor is twice or three times as large as a child, so that gesturing seems over-large and absurd. We know that some of the physicality of children is extreme but to just copy it and 'play it back' is not helpful. Just as with adult characters where stillness is required for status or at specific moments, the same dramatic rules apply. The exception is comedy: stereotypical child/teenage physicality can be used to great comic effect – even playing it back to children of the same age, who can recognise and appreciate it.

c)   Avoid clichéd child-speak – especially teen 'hip' talk.

d)   Adults can look very silly dressed as children. Do not allow designers to recreate the primary colour world of 1980s children's TV.

e)   Don't get over-anxious about playing children. It is as simple as playing any other character.

f)   Don't believe that for a play to connect with a child audience it has to ape their world; youth plays don't have to have hip-hop and rap; teenage plays don't have to have drugs, sex and violence. But they might.

g)   Don't believe that for a play to connect with young people it has to have child characters.

h)   Don't mimic children – a child's physicality in an adult's body is absurd.

i)   Don't 'hang on' to the idea that you are acting as a child. This idea should become irrelevant.

The three Acting Like Children workshops took place in spring 2011. They are part of an on-going attempt to raise the standard of theatre for young people.

Fuller documentation is available from Rose Bruford College.

OTHER THEATRES, OTHER WORLDS

PAUL HARMAN

The modern playwriting tradition of these 'Islands at the Edge of the World' as some of us call them today – with tongue in cheek – is second to none. Sorry, Messrs Molière, Chekhov, Brecht, Miller, but we think Shakespeare, Sheridan and Beckett constitute an unbeatable Olympic medal podium. And those Anglo-Irish team coaches sit behind every contemporary writer of plays for children, imposing their silent, critical authority.

But. The great Anglo-Irish tradition owes much to the way theatre was once sponsored, funded, supported by important people, made into a successful commercial industry and finally elevated to a national treasure status in both Ireland (first) and the UK (later). Forget some unique poetic genius in the English language married to a Celtic imagination. There was a demand for new plays in London and other great cities of the British Empire at its height which meant many writers could get their work staged. And they could eat.

London or Berlin?

Today Germany has a market for TYA plays much larger than in England, because of the way TYA is funded. For many years, and especially in the 70s and 80s, GRIPS Theatre company in West Berlin, supported generously from public funds but independent in spirit, produced dozens of texts which were staged world-wide from Brazil to India. These were all direct, bouncy shows which talked directly to children about the reality of their lives. They were not precious about political balance and were mostly direct attacks on conservative German mores, old-fashioned attitudes to children, disability, entitlement, race and cultural difference. *Stronger than Superman* by English writer Roy Kift was written for GRIPS for the 1981 UN Year of Disabled People and is a joyful exploration of adult prejudice and kids taking power into their own hands.

Empowerment has been the theme of GRIPS' founder and principal playwright Volker Ludwig from the start.

From 1949 to 1989, on the other side of Berlin in the German Democratic Republic, a more staid but well-resourced Theatre of Friendship (now Theater-an-der-Parkaue) was the home of many fine writers, such as Horst Hawemann. Through that stable ensemble of writers, academics, directors and administrators, TYA in many developing countries was encouraged, from Cuba to Vietnam. The tradition of a text-based theatre was faithfully transmitted, not always with lasting success, for cultural reasons. Today a united Berlin is perhaps the strongest centre of TYA activity in Europe.

In the Netherlands, Ad de Bont is one of several writers whose work has travelled successfully to be staged abroad in many other languages. *Mirad, a Boy from Bosnia, Mother Africa* and, my favourite, *Paradise Island, (Het verdronken land van Milo)* are examples. In his early years the Dutch Government was much more generous to the arts than it is now in these Austerian times. Ad de Bont has also had the advantage of his own production company, Wederzijds, with a policy of touring into schools. This is unusual in mainland Europe, where proper stage lighting and fixed seating in a darkened hall a bus ride away from school are considered by many producers to be essential elements of a quality TYA experience. With minimal scenery and technical support, the focus is on words in the actors' mouths.

Child-Centred

Like Theatre in Education in the UK, TYA in Sweden in the 1960s was the product of a Social Democratic conviction that everyone, especially children, should have access to the arts. The charismatic director of the Swedish National Theatre's TYA department, Suzanne Osten, had a unique opportunity to devote time to research into the reality of children's lives, to develop a methodology of performance with top class actors, and to stage shows without any compromise on production values.

The result was a string of really cutting edge plays like *Medea's Children*, about the consequences of divorce for children, *Toad Aquarium*, about mixed families resulting from new partnerships, and T*he Mother and the Trash*, about caring for a parent with severe mental illness. From the 1980s, Osten was a star world-wide at ASSITEJ Congresses and TYA conferences and workshops. Finally, however, the host institution pulled the plug. Times change.

Back in the USSR

The USSR can be said to have invented the idea of independent, specialist theatre institutions for young audiences, starting in the 1920's in Leningrad, now St Petersburg again. TYUZ is a contraction of the Russian for 'Theatre of the Young Spectator', and there are still, twenty-five years after the collapse of the USSR, some sixty TYUZi, with permanent professional companies and a dozen new shows joining the repertoire every year. In the old days, the play-lists of those institutions included scores of contemporary texts, dealing with social issues related to young people, alongside classics from many traditions, and fairy tale adaptations. In today's Russian theatre, dominated by commercial pressures, you will more likely find *Hairspray* in the repertoire than *Hamlet* or a new play about teenage angst. Most certainly you will not find any reference to LGBT issues or armed conflict on Russia's borders.

But note the word, spectator. Not 'Theatre *for* Young People' or 'Young People's Theatre', the popular terms in 1970s child-centred UK. The Russian and Soviet tradition was always more about transmission of the cultural heritage than use of the art form to engage young people in understanding the world around them. As a result, very few Russian plays for young audiences have ever been staged abroad. The quality of the writing is high, as the underlying tradition is so strong, but the content has rarely been in tune with contemporary Western concerns and approaches.

One other country where a standard model of a Soviet 'problem play' for teenagers was often adopted, was Japan. Some companies were heavily identified with the Communist Party of Japan and produced shows for huge audiences in which a procession of authority figures comment upon some bad behaviour by a deviant youngster. At one time, professional TYA was supported by half a million members of an association of parents, in the absence of government funding.

The opposite tendency in Japan and Korea, was to explore traditional theatre forms and folk tales. Many artists today are looking to develop and promote an indigenous cultural identity, uninfluenced by Western, perhaps more crudely speaking Americanised, popular culture.

Theatre Haram?

Across the Islamic world, theatre has great difficulty in adapting to religious conservatism, as do the arts in general. Traditional puppetry, for example, is tolerated in some communities, say Tunisia or Turkey, but has been heavily suppressed in others, as in Malaysia, where wayang kulit has Hindu associations. In Central Asia, the educated elite are still culturally Russian, but with each new generation since independence from the USSR, the streams of another cultural heritage, closer to Persia than

Russia, partly Islamic, partly secular, jostle more actively for precedence. The Silk Route was, after all, the world's main conduit of cultural diffusion for a thousand years before the Europeans re-discovered Sophocles. The region is wealthy once more and soon new cultural forms will emerge. For now, TYA as we know it hangs on by a thread … of cotton, if not silk.

In the USA a combination of commercial and cultural pressures make writing original plays for children about real, contemporary life also very difficult. Adaptations are safer. Good writers like Mary Hall Surface and Suzanne Zeder, for example, could not survive without other jobs, in academia or elsewhere.

In Australia, after many years creating work through the team devising process, the admired playwright Finnegan Kruckmeyer has emerged, and been commissioned to write plays by various UK companies.

The Word

France is home to hundreds of professional TYA Companies and a strong literary tradition. But the battle between defenders of the sacred text and insurgent devisers and dancers, object theatre manipulators and circus jugglers has largely been lost by those for whom the Word is the fount of all true Theatre.

The small number of Centres Dramatiques Nationals Enfance et Jeunesse set up in the 70s had their funding withdrawn a decade or two ago. There are now probably more writers for TYA in Belgium, Quebec and West Africa than in France. (The UK's Mike Kenny has picked up several commissions from French companies in recent years.)

Belgium is country of three languages and three distinct theatre cultures which have all hit the heights of excellence in TYA. The tiny German-speaking community produced the remarkable Agora Theatre, led by Marcel Cremer (1955–2009) which pushed the limits of imagination in TYA far beyond what was happening in Germany at the time. The Dutch language, Flemish city of Gent is home to Kopergietery, where experiments in crossover dance and theatre, or adults and children performing together, have challenged many traditional approaches in form and content. And to relish the profusion of innovative companies in Francophone Wallonie, a visit to the Noël au Théâtre festival and Montagne Magique in Bruxelles is a must.

And what of the inheritors of Lope de Vega and the vast human and intellectual basin of Spanish language culture in Latin America? Political upheavals and divisions, coupled with severe economic and political constraints, may have stopped playwrights in Cuba, Spain, Mexico, Colombia or Argentina reaching young audiences elsewhere in the World of TYA. In Brazil hundreds of TYA companies are active but few if any play texts have been seen abroad. Perhaps the tyranny of the English language and a focus on Europe in ASSITEJ are to blame.

But there may be different reasons.

After the social upheavals of 1968, politically challenging movements in TYA sprang up in Germany, Denmark, Belgium, France and elsewhere in Europe. Denmark and Francophone Belgium (Wallonie), for example, produce a great number of innovative and engaging new shows for young people but these are often not based on texts.

Collaboration

Many of the post-68 new wave of producers, in Europe and in many other parts of the world, operated on the fringes of officially recognised and funded structures. The actors did not come from elite conservatoires. They were political activists often working in co-operatives, with a collaborative ethos, learning on the job.

Or they simply could not afford to pay a writer and so shows were devised by the cast and never recorded.

In some countries, the cultural dominance of dance and visual theatre means that a formal text will always be a smaller, complementary element in the performance event. But across the World among those who mediate access for young people to the arts and education there is another divide. For some, a formal play for children to watch is considered less beneficial to their social, aesthetic, cultural and intellectual development than participatory theatre or the use of drama methods to explore the world. That debate is exemplified in the existence of two world organisations, IDEA and ASSITEJ.

It is however noteworthy that many UK pioneers in drama in education, like Brian Way or one of the founders of ASSITEJ, the Drama Adviser Gerald Tyler and John Allen, Her Majesty's Inspector of Drama in Schools, regarded watching a theatre performance as an equally essential experience for children.

In Italy, theatre as an expression of the individual artist's view of the world, traditional puppetry and child-centred theatre experiences co-exist somewhat uncomfortably. Given the strong regional and political differences in Italy, and the individual character of its great cities, some TYA companies are closely identified with and influenced by the cultural and political tradition of their location.

Small Size

Thirty years ago in Bologna, artist and director Roberto Frabetti founded a company called la Baracca. He soon felt the need to create a centre for children's arts. Later Frabetti created the annual festival, 'Visioni di futuro, visioni di teatro', with a focus on theatre for the very young.

Not far from Bologna, in Reggio Emilia, the local authority promoted an educational philosophy based on the image of the child as possessing strong potential for development and as a subject of rights who learns and grows in relationship with others. The practice of maintaining pre-schools up to the age of 7 in which all kinds of artistic and scientific exploration were encouraged through play was very influential for a time internationally. In some countries, formal education starts much earlier than many experts in child development regard as appropriate.

Small Size was set up in 2005 by specialists in theatre for the very young, 0–6 years. Roberto Frabetti and colleagues in Belgium, Spain and Slovenia received a significant grant from EU cultural funds which was extended from 2009 to 2014 as Small Size, Big Citizens, to enable it to become a Europe-wide network (www.smallsize.org).

Small Size asserts the importance of creating theatre which respects the needs of the child at each stage of development while presenting challenges to explore new worlds of experience.

The UK partner in Small Size is Polka Theatre, where it has been managed and cherished in a remarkable way by Jo Belloli.

Polka in turn works alongside Sticky Fingers (Newry, Northern Ireland), Starcatchers (Edinburgh, Scotland) and Theatre Hullabaloo (Darlington).

Over the last fifty years, across Europe, political and social engagement has been a feature of TYA. To decide to devote energy to the creation of festivals, networks, associations, to seek out audiences in disadvantaged neighbourhoods, to represent the interests of the voiceless, the very young or those with disabilities, is a political choice.

Do Children Prefer Bad Art?

In the UK, the Arts Council, our arms-length, government-funded agency supporting professional arts, abandoned the idea of financial support for a 'specialist' TYA after only a few years of experimental funding.

In transferring responsibility for funding theatre (and all the arts) for children to the then Ministry of Education, the justifying phrase was; "There is only good or bad theatre." The assumption was that theatre aimed at and influenced by the needs and interests of young people could not attain the same quality as that created for adults.

While in the USSR the pay rate for writing a play for children was higher than that for adults, in the UK the rate is lower, mainly because shows are shorter. While Germany has a dozen literary agencies which specialise in promoting plays for young audiences, in the UK there are none. While in Germany or Russia around 50 specialist TYA companies have their own theatre building with permanent staff, in the UK only a handful currently do.

In the 2000s, for a time, 'Creativity' became the watch word and vast amounts of money were spent on projects and programmes, ostensibly to get teachers to create art with children in 'Creative Partnerships' with professional artists. While some theatre and dance companies jumped on this funding bandwagon as it rolled its brief and rickety way, sometimes crushing a rare bloom or delicate seedling as it went, it soon ran out of fuel (money) and fell apart. The UK has never been good at consistency in arts policy. Except in always spending the biggest single amount of its cash on the elite Royal Opera House in London!

At the End of the Day

While it would be comforting to think that good artists are immune to pressure from institutional structures and make the plays they want from purity of commitment, they also have to pay their bills.

More to the purpose, there must be steady demand from professional companies with secure audiences to justify adding to the long list of good plays for young audiences that have been written and produced in the last fifty years.

In the UK we are fortunate in having a number of writers who learned their craft in times when security of employment, as part of an ensemble, was underpinned by public funding. In the current era of austerity such opportunities are fewer.

Let's celebrate their achievements while we may.

End Note

Detail on TYA in the member countries of ASSITEJ, from China to Peru, Iceland to Zimbabwe, can be found through the ASSITEJ Playwrights network, Write Local. Play Global.

This an online meeting place, run by Peter Kim Kovak, USA and Tony Mack, Australia – on both Facebook and on our website – for people interested in work written for young audiences. It may be considered a virtual café where one can read about, make contact and catch up with people from around the world. There is information about exciting new work, how writers approach their craft and about organizations that support and develop the work of writers for young audiences.

Links:

assitej-international.org/en/

writelocalplayglobal.org/

THANK YOU, LYN GARDNER

NINA HAJIYIANNI

Every art movement needs critics, reviewers and fans. Today we have bloggers and vloggers as well as online and traditional theatre critics. TYA benefits enormously from those who can seriously evaluate the work and make it known to wider audiences. Regular informed criticism can help practitioners to improve their artistic practice through receiving thoughtful feedback as well as allowing those in the same field to be made aware of new ideas, forms and styles. When reviews are published in national newspapers, the movement gains respect and credibility in the eyes of the general public as well as encouraging ticket sales. Reviews also help to raise the profile of playwrights working in the field of Theatre for Young Audiences, writers who are often overlooked in discussions of Children's Literature. In 2012, Susan Elkin made a wonderfully bold proposal when she called for the next Children's Laureate to be a playwright, nominating David Wood for the post. https://www.thestage.co.uk/opinion/2012/a-playwright-for-the-next-childrens-laureate-please/

Theatre for Young Audiences has had numerous reviewers and critics over the last half century but none more committed to following and commenting on the movement's progress than Lyn Gardner, *Guardian* Theatre Critic.

In 2013, Lyn Gardner received an Action for Children's Arts (ACA) Award for Outstanding Contribution to Children's Arts, for her coverage of TYA. Nina Hajiyianni is Artistic

Director of Action Transport Theatre and Chair of TYA-UK Centre of ASSITEJ and this is the speech she gave at the award:

"Thank you for inviting me here today to say some words about Lyn Gardner's contribution to children's theatre and her 'outstanding achievement to children's arts.'

I made a list of all the things I think Lyn Gardner champions:
- practice that pushes the boundaries of art
- young and emerging artists
- newness
- found spaces and art in surprising places
- surprise
- risk
- audience and artist blur – that is, who is who?
- independence
- story
- fun
- meaning

And these are the things that I think Lyn Gardner doesn't like:
- boring work
- unskilled practice
- 'the past at the sake of the future' quote/unquote.

And I could say 'children's theatre' to both the things that Lyn champions and the things she doesn't like.

Because 'Children's Theatre' is not one thing and the term often instils an assumption that it is 'generic' or worse, synonymous with bad art… theatre which is 'dumbed down' for its audience.

We know that Children's Theatre is a term which implies that a performance has thought about its audience. Often it is *more* imaginative than other theatre because of it.

But the art can be good or bad.

And this is what Lyn promotes, the idea that work for young audience can be stunning, awe inspiring, ground-breaking, like any other 'best work' and it can also be bad. But it is worthy of the same artistic rigour, judgement, study and critique as any other art. Lyn judges assuming the best is possible and by this assumption, helps raise the bar.

However, it is important now, perhaps more than ever, that theatre for children as a 'movement' is seen as necessary. That we understand that theatre offers children the chance to experience something 'other'. To enter a space that is different to any other they know. Where ideas and expression occur; where emotions and intellect are connected; where children tap into their own curiosity and judgement.

Lyn helps us *know* this work. She shares her own insights and promotes work for children and companies which make work for children.

Even work that happens outside of London. There are precious few people with sound artistic insights doing that.

To quote one of the comments referring to Lyn's weekly theatre blog: 'In an age of such widespread, instant opinion – you need someone you can rely on.'

Thank you, Lyn Gardner."

End Note

In 2015, to celebrate the 50th anniversary of TIE, Mike Kenny and Charles Way both received the ACA Trustees' Award for their contribution to TYA playwriting.

USEFUL RESOURCES

Publishers and Literary Agents

Alan Brodie Representation www.alanbrodie.com
Anchorage Press, USA www.anchoragepress.com
Aurora Metro Books www.aurorametro.com
Casarotto Ramsay Marsh www.casarotto.co.uk
Collins Educational www.collins.co.uk
Dramatic Lines Publishers www.dramaticlines.co.uk
Faber and Faber www.faber.co.uk
Felicity Trew www..carolinesheldon.co.uk
Knight Hall Agency www.knighthallagency.com
MBA Literary Agents www.mbalit.co.uk
Methuen Books www.methuen.co.uk
Nick Hern Books www.nickhernbooks.co.uk
Oberon Books www.oberonbooks.com
Samuel French Ltd www.samuelfrench.com
The Agency www.theagency.co.uk
United Agents, Giles Smart gsmart@unitedagents.co.uk

Playwrights on the Web

Neil Duffield www.homepage.ntlworld.com/n.duffield1/
Andrea Earl www.tutti-frutti.org.uk/show/the-girl-who-lost-her-smile/
David Holman www.doollee.com/PlaywrightsH/holman-david.html
Mike Kenny www.playsforyoungaudiences.org/playwrights/mike-kenny
Vicky Ireland www.vickyireland.com

USEFUL RESOURCES

Brian Way www.samuelfrench.com/author/3728/brian-way
Charles Way www.charles-way.co.uk/#

Books for Further Reading

Learning through Theatre: The Changing Face of Theatre in Education, Anthony Jackson and Chris Vine (eds), (Routledge), 2013. 340 pp. ISBN 978-0-415-53071-2.

Oily Cart: All Sorts of Theatre for All Sorts of Kids, M. Brown (ed), (Trentham Books), 2012.

Theatre, Education and Performance: The Map and the Story, Helen Nicholson, (Palgrave Macmillan), 2011. 245 pp. ISBN 978-0-230-57423-6.

Contemporary Theatre in Education, Roger Wooster, (Intellect), 2007. 176 pp. ISBN 978-1-84150-170-3

Theatre, Education and the Making of Meanings, Anthony Jackson, (Manchester University Press), 2007. 310 pp. ISBN 978-0-7190-6543-9

Theatre for Children and Young People, Stuart Bennett (ed), (Aurora Metro), 2005. 244 pp. ISBN 978-0-9546912-8-8. Provides case notes written by leading professionals in the field covering all aspects of making, writing and delivering theatre for young audiences today in the UK.

Theatre for Children – A Guide to Writing, Adapting, Directing and Acting, David Wood with Janet Grant, (Faber), 1997. 248 pp. ISBN 0-571-17749-2. Wood's approach to making his own famous brand of building based theatre.

Taking Issue: Three Playwrights and a Theatre Company, Theatre Company Blah Blah Blah, (Alumnus Press). ISBN 1-901-439-03-8.

Theatre for the Young, Alan England, (Macmillan Education), 1990. 244 pp. ISBN 0-333-35082-0. Useful exploration of definitions and genres, such as traditional, fantasy, social realism with international references.

Exploring Theatre & Education, Ken Robinson (ed), (Heinemann), 1980. 191 pp. ISBN 0-435-18780-5.

Theatre in Education: New Objectives for Theatre, New Techniques in Education, John O'Toole, (Hodder and Stoughton), 1976. 168 pp. ISBN 0-340-20618-7. The first full-length study of the theory and practice of TIE. Contains photos of early participatory programmes.

Actors in Schools: Education Survey, No. 22, Bert Parnaby, HMI (HMSO), 1976. 74 pp. Detailed recommendations on how teachers should prepare to receive TIE teams in schools.

TIE Texts

Playing Out, Eirwen Hopkins (ed), (Argraff), 2005. 322 pp. ISBN 1-85596-663-8. Introduction to TIE in Wales with texts of eight plays.

Plays for Children. Helen Rose (ed), (Faber & Faber), 2000. 276 pp. ISBN 0-571-20339-6. Four play scripts: *Indigo Mill* by Nick Fisher, *Body Talk* by Andy Rashleigh, *Odessa & the Magic Goat* by John Agard and *Little Victories* by Shaun Prendergast.

Six Theatre-in-Education Programmes, Christine Redington (ed), (Methuen), 1987. 140 pp. ISBN 0-413-15790-3. Texts of: *Dirty Rascals* (Leeds TIE), *Peacemaker*, *Under Exposure* (Theatre Centre), *The School on the Green* (Greenwich Young People's Theatre), *Questions Arising from a Mutiny in 1789* (Action PIE, Cardiff), *Lives Worth Living* (Belgrade TIE).

Raj, Leeds Playhouse TIE, (Amber Lane Press), 1984.

Theatre in Education: Four Junior Programmes, Pam Schweitzer (ed), (Eyre Methuen), 1980. 236 pp. by ISBN 0-413-40190-1. Texts of *The Price of Coal* (Belgrade TIE), *Rubbish* (Leeds TIE), *Travellers* (Lancaster TIE), and *Big Deal* (Belgrade TIE). Also in Methuen Young Drama; *Theatre in Education: Five Infant Programmes* and *Theatre in Education: Four Secondary Programmes*.

Sweetie Pie: A Play About Women in Society, devised by Bolton Octagon TIE in 1972, introduction by Eileen Murphy, (Methuen Young Drama), 1975. 82 pp. ISBN 0-413-33670-0. This is a detailed description of Theatre in Education methods.

UK Government Policy, Reports and White Papers

1965: White Paper: *A Policy for the Arts: The First Steps*. Jennie Lee MP. Proposed increase in Government financial support for the Arts.

1970: Arts Council Theatre Enquiry. Chair W.E. Williams.

1976: *Support for the Arts in England & Wales*. Lord Redcliffe Maud. See pp. 120 et seq. on TYP.

1978: "Spending on the arts in UK: 50p per head. Sweden: £4; Germany: £7."

1983: NADECT Journal Outlook November: Focus on TIE with articles by David Johnston et al.

1984: *Glory of the Garden*. Arts Council.

1984: *Arts in Schools*. Ken Robinson.

1985: *Theatre and Education Conference Report*. Arts Council, ed. Ken Robinson.

1986: *A Policy for Theatre for Young People*. Arts Council, ed. Sian Ede.

1986: *Theatre is for All*. Report of Enquiry chaired by Sir Kenneth Cork. See pp. 36–37 on Theatre for Young People.

1999: *Culture and Education in England 1999*. Tony Graham on Unicorn Theatre's 50th anniversary. In Education and Social Justice.

1999: *All Our Futures; Creativity, Culture & Education*. Report of Committee chaired by Prof. Ken Robinson.

2015: *Step by Step: Arts Policy and Young People 1944–2014*. Culture at Kings (Kings College, London). Detailed historical review of policies on access for young people to the arts.

2016: Culture White Paper.

International Publications

Belgium

Théâtre et Education dans le monde 2015, (Lansman – ANRAT – IDEA) Papers from IDEA 2013 conference, Paris.

Le Petit Cyrano (on-line periodical published by CTEJ) www.ctej. be/le-petit-cyrano/

Theatres en Mouvement, Jeanne Pigeon, (Les Cahiers du Soleil Debout), 1990. ISSN 0395-6784 An account of the evolution of five key European companies since 1968; Teatro dell'Angolo (Turin, Italy), Theatre Des Jeunes Annees (Lyon, France), GRIPS Theater (Berlin, Germany) Theatre de la Guimbarde (Belgium) and Teatro O Bando (Portugal).

France

Les Ravisseurs d'enfants, Maurice Yendt, (Actes Sud-Papiers), Paris, 1989. 175 pp. ISBN 2-86943-200-3 Account of the author's work at the Theatre des Jeunes Annees, Lyon, 1968–1989. Most influential figure in theatre for young audiences in France during this period, especially through the programme of the biennial festival (RITEJ) organised by TJA.

USA

Discovering a New Audience for Theatre, Nat Eek, (Sunstone Press), 2008. 348 pp. ISBN: 978-0-86534-660-4 First of three volumes tracing the 65 year history of ASSITEJ (1965–2015).

Expanding the New Audience for Theatre, Nat Eek, (Sunstone Press). 380 pp. ISBN: 978-0-86534-798-4

Maintaining the New Audience for Theatre, Nat Eek, (Sunstone Press), 2014. ISBN: 978-0-86534-987-2

Children's Theatre: A Selected and Annotated Bibliography, Wesley VanTassel, (Rowman & Littlefield), 1975. 38 pp.

Germany

Theater für Kinder und Jugendliche: Beiträge zu Theorie und Praxis, Wolfgang Schneider, (Georg Olms), 2012. 468 pp ISBN-10: 3-487-14832-3; ISBN-13: 978-3-487-14832-8. German text; reviews twenty-five years of development of TYA in Germany by founder of ASSITEJ Germany and leading academic commentator on TYA and cultural policy.

The Archive and Library of the German National Centre for Theatre for Children and Young People (www.kjtz.de) is in Frankfurt-am-Main. It is an extensive collection including play texts in many languages, magazines, books and publicity material, probably the largest in the world.

For over twenty years, the publication *Grimm & Grips* recorded plays produced and other activities of every professional TYA company in Germany.

One series of books produced by the Centre introduced German readers to work in other countries. Others focused on topics such as Youth Theatre or theatre for the very young.

The Centre also houses the archive of ASSITEJ and fifty years of publications, reports, records of conferences, Congresses and festivals in over 80 countries on every continent, and organises an annual Playwright's Forum, to introduce new authors to potential producers.

Research in TIE and TYA

For research in this field, the *Research in Drama Education* (RiDE) journal, published quarterly by Routledge, is a good source.

Various research articles on TIE and YPT by Prof. Joe Winston and Prof. Matthew Reason are worth looking out for., but see especially:

'Ideology, practice and evaluation: developing the effectiveness of theatre in education', G. Allen, I. Allen, I. and L. Dalrymple, (1999). RiDE 4.1, pp. 21–36.

'You had to watch it to realise what it were like': researching audiences for educational theatre. A. Jackson, (2002), in *Playing Betwixt and Between: the IDEA dialogues*, Bjørn Rasmussen and Anna-Lena Østern (eds). (IDEA Publications), Bergen, 2001. pp. 168–77.

'Targets, outcomes – and playfulness.' A. Jackson, (2007), Chapter 8 in *Theatre, Education and the Making of Meanings* (Manchester University Press), 2007. pp. 198–232.

'Seeing it for real...?': authenticity, theatre and learning in museums.' A. Jackson and H. Rees Leahy, (2005). RiDE 10.3, pp. 303–25.

Theatre, Education and Performance: The Map and the Story, H. Nicholson, (Palgrave Macmillan), 2011.

Performance and Participation: Practices, Audiences, Politics, H. Nicholson, and A. Harpin, (eds), (Palgrave Macmillan), 2106.

The Young Audience: Exploring and Enhancing Children's Experiences of Theatre, M. Reason, (Trentham), 2010.

'Between the aesthetic and the ethical: analysing the tension at the heart of theatre in education', J. Winston, (2005). Journal of Moral Education, 34.3, pp. 309–23.

Beauty and Education, J. Winston, (Routledge), 2011.

Plus a selection here, for browsing through: www.tandfonline. com/action/showMostReadArticles?journalCode=crde20

Further Study

University MA courses in TYA are offered at Worcester, Rose Bruford and Bath Spa Universities (see also www.scudd.org.uk).

ITYARN (International Theatre for Young Audiences Research Network) is the international research network of ASSITEJ International (see www.ityarn.org).

Archives

A project to map the archives of TIE companies, currently held at a number of locations, has been launched (Facebook page: Archiving Theatre in Education – www.facebook.com/ groups/858571770865233/).

A number of collections related to ASSITEJ, UK Drama, TIE and TYA are held in the archive of Arizona State University, USA (www.asu.edu).

UK TYA COMPANIES & FESTIVALS

This list of over 170 organisations identified in 2016 includes larger producing theatres which stage some plays for young audiences, presenting venues, festivals and other supporting organisations, and independent touring companies which create productions for young audiences.

Companies which are members of the TYA-UK Centre of ASSITEJ (www.tya-uk.org) are marked with (A) and companies or organisations which are NPO's, (National Portfolio Organisations) in receipt of regular financial assistance from Arts Councils in Wales, Scotland, Northern Ireland or England are marked with (NPO). For more details see www.artscouncil.org.uk

20 Stories High, Liverpool 20storieshigh.org.uk (A, NPO)

Action Transport, Ellesmere Port
actiontransporttheatre.co.uk (A, NPO)

Actionwork TIE, Devon actionwork.com (A)

Aesops Touring Theatre Company, Woking
aesopstheatre.co.uk

Agor Drysau Festival, Aberystwyth, Wales aradgoch.org

AJTC, Guildford ajtctheatre.co.uk (A)

Alive and Kicking, Leeds
aliveandkickingtheatrecompany.co.uk

Ambassador Theatre Group, London atg.co.uk (A)

Antic Theatre, Swansea, Wales antictheatre.co.uk

Ape Theatre Company, London apetheatrecompany.co.uk

Arad Goch, Aberystwyth, Wales aradgoch.org (A)
ARC Theatre Ensemble, London arctheatre.com
Arkeen, Motherwell, Scotland arkeen.co.uk

Bamboozle, Leicester bamboozletheatre.co.uk
Barking Dog Theatre Company, Hertfordshire
  barkingdog.co.uk
Belfast Children's Festival, Belfast, Northern Ireland (A)
Big Brum Theatre In Education, Birmingham
  bigbrum.org.uk
Big Fish, Greenwich, London bigfishtheatre.co.uk
Big Wheel TIE, London bigwheel.org.uk
Big Window Theatre, East Midlands
  bigwindowtheatre.com
Big Wooden Horse, London bigwoodenhorse.com
Birmingham Rep, Birmingham
  birmingham-rep.co.uk (A, NPO)
Bitesize Theatre, Wrexham, Wales bitesizetheatre.co.uk
Black Box Theatre, Liverpool blackboxmerseyside.co.uk
Black Cat Theatre Company, South East
  blackcat-theatre.co.uk/
Blue Sky Theatre Company, Coventry blueskytheatre.com
Blunderbus Theatre, Newark blunderbus.co.uk
Booster Cushion Theatre, London
  booster-cushion.co.uk (A)
Box Clever, London boxclevertheatre.com
Bristol Old Vic, Bristol bristololdvic.org.uk (A, NPO)
BZ Ents, Leicestershire, East Midlands bzents.co.uk

Cahoots NI, Belfast, Northern Ireland cahootsni.com (A)
Cascade, Truro cascadetheatre.co.uk
Catherine Wheels, Edinburgh, Scotland
  catherinewheels.co.uk (A)
C'est Tous Shakespeare Theatre Company, North West
  saytwo.co.uk
Channel Theatre Company, Margate channel-theatre.co.uk
Classworks Theatre, Cambridge classworks.org.uk

Clwyd Theatr Cymru, Mold, Wales ctctyp.co.uk (A, NPO)
Clyde Built Puppets, Scotland clydebuiltpuppet.co.uk
Company of Angels, London
  companyofangels.co.uk (A, NPO)
Complete Works, London tcw.org.uk
Coventry Belgrade Theatre, Coventry
  belgrade.co.uk (A, NPO)
Cragrats, Holmfirth, Yorkshire cragrats.com
Creu Cymru, Aberystwyth, Wales creucumru.com (A)
Cwmni'r Fran Wen, Menai Bridge, Wales franwen.com

Daylight Theatre, Stroud lipstress.wix.com/daylight
D. N. A., North West dynamicnewanimation.co.uk (A)

the egg, Bath theatreroyal.org.uk/page/3030/the+egg (A)

Fevered Sleep, London feveredsleep.co.uk (A)
Firehorse, Port Talbot, Wales firehorsetheatre.com
Fizz Theatre Company, London fizztheatre.org.uk
Floods of Ink, South East floodsofink.com
Flying Theatre Company, Yorkshire flyingtheatre.com
Freehand Theatre, Shipley freehandtheatre.co.uk (A)
Full House, Bedfordshire fullhouse.org.uk (A)

Gaga Theatre, South East gagatheatre.co.uk
Garlic Theatre, Norwich garlictheatre.org.uk (A)
Gazebo TIE, Darlaston gazebotie.org
Gibber Training, Newcastle gibber.org
Globe Players, London
  rcsherrifftrust.org.uk/website/recartists/globep.htm
Greenwich & Lewisham YPT, London glypt.co.uk
Gwent Theatre, Abergavenny, Wales gwenttheatre.com (A)

Half Moon YPT, London halfmoon.org.uk (A)
Hand To Mouth, Southampton handtomouth.co.uk (A)
Hanyong Theatre, Birmingham hanyong.co.uk
Hiccup Theatre, Farnham hiccuptheatre.co.uk
Hobgoblin Theatre Company
  hobgoblintheatrecompany.co.uk

50 BEST PLAYS

Hoopla Theatre, Birmingham hooplatheatre.com (A)
Hopscotch, Glasgow, Scotland hopscotchtheatre.com
Hurricane Productions Ltd., London
  hurricaneproductions.co.uk

Ian Saville, London redmagic.co.uk/savillemagic/
Illyria, Cornwall illyria.uk.com
Image Musical Theatre, London
  imagemusicaltheatre.co.uk
Imaginate, Edinburgh, Scotland imaginate.org.uk/festival
Indefinite Articles, Cambridge
  facebook.com/Indefinite-Articles-Theatre-Co
Intext Performance, South East
  intextperformance.com (A)

Jack Drum Arts, Bishop Auckland jackdrum.co.uk (A)

Kazzum, London kazzum.org (A)
Kinetic, London kinetictheatre.co.uk
Konflux Theatre, Yorkshire konfluxtheatre.com
Krazy Kat, Brighton krazykattheatre.co.uk

Lambeth Children's Theatre Company, London
  lambch@globalnet.co.uk (A)
Language Alive, Birmingham theplayhouse.org.uk
Leeds TIE, Leeds leedstie.blogspot.com
Legend Theatre, London legendtheatre.com
Licketyspit, Scotland licketyspit.com
Little Angel, London littleangeltheatre.com
Little Feet Festival, York yorktheatreroyal.co.uk
Live Wire Productions, Scotland
  livewireproductions.org.uk
London Drama, London londondrama.org (A)
Loud Mouth, Birmingham loudmouth.co.uk
Lynx Theatre in Education lynne.kentish@talk21.com

M&M, Ayr, Scotland magicoftheatre.com
M6 Theatre, Rochdale m6theatre.co.uk (A, NPO)
Magic Attic, Worcester d.broster@worc.ac.uk

UK TYA COMPANIES AND FESTIVALS

Magic Carpet Theatre, Hull magiccarpettheatre.com (A)
Mess Up the Mess, Ammanford, Wales
   messupthemess.co.uk (A)
Mimika, Leeds, Yorkshire mimikatheatre.com (A)
Moby Duck, Birmingham moby-duck.co.uk
Multistory Theatre, Barnstaple multistorytheatre.co.uk
Myrtle Theatre Company myrtletheatrecompany.co.uk

New International Encounters, Cambridge
   nie-theatre.com (A)

No Limits Theatre, Sunderland nolimitstheatre.org.uk

Oily Cart, London oilycart.org.uk (A, NPO)
Onatti Theatre Company, Coventry onatti.co.uk

Pals Productions, Hertfordshire palsproductions.co.uk
Pandemonium Theatre, Cardiff
   pandemoniumtheatre.co.uk
Paper Balloon, London paperballoon.org.uk (A)
Paradox Theatre paradoxtheatre.co.uk
Peut Etre, London peutetretheatre.co.uk (A)
Pied Piper, Guildford piedpipertheatre.co.uk
Pilot Theatre Company, Wakefield
   pilot-theatre.net (NPO)
Playtime Theatre Company, Whitstable
   playtimetheatre.co.uk (A)
Pocketful of Nothing, London
   pocketfulofnothing.com (A)
Polka Theatre, London polkatheatre.com (A, NPO)
Prime Theatre, Swindon sixthsensetheatre.com
Proper Job Theatre Company, Huddersfield
   properjob.org.uk

Quantum Theatre for Science, London
   quantumtheatre.co.uk

Red Earth, Derby redearththeatre.com (NPO)
Red Ladder, Leeds redladder.co.uk
Replay, Belfast, NI replaytheatreco.org (A, NPO)

Rhubarb Theatre, Lincoln rhubarbtheatre.co.uk
Rose Bruford College, Sidcup bruford.ac.uk (A)

Scarabeus, London scarabeus.co.uk
Second Hand Dance, London secondhanddance.co.uk (A)
Shakespeare 4 Kidz, South East shakespeare4kidz.com
Sherman Cymru, Cardiff, Wales shermancymru.co.uk (A)
Shona Reppe, Scotland shonareppe.co.uk
Small World Theatre, Wales smallworld.org.uk
Solomon Associates, Hampshire solomontheatre.co.uk
Sonsie Music, Scotland sonsiemusic.co.uk
Spacefund, Canterbury spacefund.co.uk
Spark Festival, Leicestershire sparkfestival.co.uk (A, NPO)
Spectacle Theatre, Wales spectacletheatre.co.uk
Starcatchers, Edinburgh, Scotland starcatchers.org.uk
Storytellers Theatre, Blackpool pendleproductions.co.uk

TAG Theatre Company, Glasgow, Scotland
Take-away Theatre, Scotland takeawaytheatre.co.uk
Takeoff Festival, Durham takeofffestival.org.uk
Tall Stories, London tallstories.org.uk (A)
Tam Tam Theatre, London tamtamtheatre.co.uk
Tangere Arts, East Midlands tangere-arts.co.uk/wp/ (A)
Tara Arts, London tara-arts.com
Team Players, Middlesbrough
Tell Tale Hearts, Leeds telltalehearts.co.uk (A)
The People's Theatre Company, Surrey ptc.org.uk
Theatr Iolo, Cardiff, Wales theatriolo.com (A, NPO)
Theatr na n'Og, Neath, Wales theatr-nanog.co.uk (A)
Theatre Alibi, Exeter theatrealibi.co.uk (A, NPO)
Theatre Centre, London theatre-centre.co.uk (A, NPO)
Theatre Company Blah Blah Blah, Leeds
   blahs.co.uk (A, NPO)
Theatre Exchange, Caterham
   info@theatre-exchange.org.uk
Theatre Hullabaloo, Darlington
   theatrehullabaloo.org.uk (A, NPO)

UK TYA COMPANIES AND FESTIVALS

Theatre Rites, London theatre-rites.co.uk (A, NPO)
Theatre sans Frontieres, Hexham tsf.org.uk (A)
Thousand Cranes, London athousandcranes.org.uk (A)
Ticklish Allsorts, Salisbury ticklishallsorts.co.uk
TIE Tours, Somerset tietours.com
TPP, Llanelli, Wales tpptheatricalproductions.co.uk
Travelling Light, Bristol
   travellinglighttheatre.org.uk (A, NPO)
Travelling Storyteller, Chesterfield
   travelling-storyteller.com
Tutti Frutti, Leeds tutti-frutti.co.uk (A, NPO)

Unicorn Theatre, London unicorntheatre.com (A, NPO)
Unity Theatre, Liverpool
   unitytheatreliverpool.co.uk (A, NPO)

Visible Fictions, Edinburgh, Scotland
   visiblefictions.co.uk (A)
Visitation Productions, North East
   visitationproductions.co.uk

Walk the Plank, Salford (Ship) walktheplank.co.uk
Warwick Arts Centre, Warwick warwickartscentre.co.uk (A)
Watershed, Stockport watershedtheatre.com
Wee Stories, Edinburgh, Scotland weestoriestheatre.org
West Yorkshire Playhouse, Leeds wyp.org.uk (A, NPO)
Westcountry Theatre, Torquay w-t-c.co.uk
Whirlwind Theatre Productions, Lancaster
   whirlwindtheatre.org.uk
Whisper & Shout, Gloucester whisperandshout.co.uk
Winter Walker, Derbyshire winterwalker.org.uk (A)

Y Touring, London ytouring.myresourcecloud.net
Yellow Earth, London yellowearth.org
Young at Art, Belfast, Northern Ireland youngatart.co.uk (A)
Young Vic, London youngvic.org (A, NPO)

THE FUTURE

VICKY IRELAND

The TIE movement has sadly dwindled in England and morphed into the more general TYA, with only a few specialist pockets still remaining, but one of its legacies is the idea that outreach is vital and this in turn has led to the creation of the Education Officer and Education Departments in all our major arts institutions and organisations. Something to be very proud of.

In order to further develop TYA England we really need bold initiatives to stimulate and encourage new work. One brilliant example is the egg's pioneering Incubator programme which aims to develop world class theatre for young audiences and is now in its third year. Funded by The Leverhulme Trust and The Esmée Fairbairn Foundation between 2014 and 2017, The Incubator programme selects artists and theatre companies from across the British Isles and provides optimal conditions for them to experiment in and create new plays. The aim of the programme is to encourage more talented artists to write and make plays for young audiences and ensure this work is the best it can be.

Equally bold and visionary is Rose Bruford College's annual project, called DREAM: "The Joy of Creating, will promote the performing arts to children and young people and provide opportunities for them to participate in, see and create new works, and influence the development of professional practitioners." The project is led by Jeremy Harrison, who is Programme Director (dreamkent@bruford.ac.uk).

Sadly ACE no longer funds Theatre Centre's Brian Way TYA New Writing Award. Although often considered controversial, awards can serve to foster the playwright and their play and bring our work to the attention of the media, giving much-needed publicity. Perhaps we need a new one?

There are some splendid festivals in England, but a London-based showcase of new and scratch work for Young People and Children could raise our profile and encourage programmers to programme more English work.

Likewise we need representation at many more artistic tables and at award ceremonies where no-one is invited to represent children's theatre and there are no categories to celebrate our work.

We need to show our support for the Drama Theatre and Young People Manifesto, which sets out all the benefits to children of theatre and drama, by placing a link on our websites. www.dramatheatremanifesto.co.uk

We currently have an English government which finds it difficult to acknowledge the importance and place of the arts within the curriculum or to encourage schools to both book in artistic events and organise trips out during school time to visit them. Because of this more and more children will be deprived of artistic experiences. It could well learn from the Scottish government who recently decided to implement *The Theatre in Schools Scotland Initiative* which aims "to ensure that every child experiences a minimum of one performing arts production per year as part of their education."

Well done Scotland!

In conclusion, despite the problems of funding, the cost of production budgets, the fear of programming the unknown title, the reduction of cast sizes, the re-formatting from two acts to one act, the lack of commitment by the present government to the place of the arts in the curriculum, – alongside adaptations of books and well-known stories, we hope theatres and companies will continue to foster writers and commission new original plays for children and young people.

We all need theatre and drama in our lives and as long as there are those individuals who care passionately about sharing the world's stories and the big questions of life with our young people, we have no doubt that ways will be found to nurture brilliant new English playwrights and plays.

So pick up your pen and start!